200
STUDENT MEALS

D0550166

HAMLYN **ALL COLOUR COOKBOOK**

200

STUDENT MEALS

SARA LEWIS

An Hachette UK Company
www.hachette.co.uk

First published in Great Britain in 2011 by Hamlyn,
a division of Octopus Publishing Group Ltd,
Carmelite House, 50 Victoria Embankment,
London EC4Y 0DZ
www.octopusbooks.co.uk

This edition published in 2016

ISBN 978-0-600-63340-2

A CIP catalogue record for this book is available
from the British Library

Printed and bound in China

10 9 8 7 6 5 4 3 2 1

Standard level spoon measurement are used in all recipes.
1 tablespoon = one 15 ml spoon
1 teaspoon = one 5 ml spoon

Both imperial and metric measures have been given in
all recipes. Use one set of measurements only and not a
mixture of both.

Eggs should be medium unless otherwise stated. The
Department of Health advises that eggs should not be
consumed raw. This book contains dishes made with raw
or lightly cooked eggs. It is prudent for more vulnerable
people such as pregnant and nursing mothers, invalids,
the elderly, babies and young children to avoid uncooked
or lightly cooked dishes made with eggs. Once prepared
these dishes should be kept refrigerated and used
promptly.

Ovens should be preheated to the specific temperature
– if using a fan-assisted oven, follow the manufacturer's
instructions for adjusting the time and the temperature.

This book includes dishes made with nuts and nut
derivatives. It is advisable for customers with known
allergic reactions to nuts and nut derivatives and those who
may be potentially vulnerable to these allergies, such as
pregnant and nursing mothers, invalids, the elderly, babies
and children, to avoid dishes made with nuts and nut
oils. It is also prudent to check the labels of pre-prepared
ingredients for the possible inclusion of nut derivatives.

contents

introduction

introduction

Student food needn't be dull, just because you are on a tight budget. You might have to plan a little more so that the money you do have can go as far as possible but that is perhaps the hardest bit. Anyone can cook and with so many influences from around the world, student food can be as traditional or as exotic as you want it. Gradually build up a store cupboard of favourite spices and ingredients you use a lot (see opposite for some ideas) and then pick up fresh food as and when you need it.

essentials to take to college

cooking equipment

You don't need to spend a packet to get a basic set of cooking things together. Supermarkets and large department stores have a wide range of basic items and the chances are that your family will have extra pots and pans to donate. Try local charity shops for bargains, or students who are moving on, who might also want to sell on their items.

tools and implements

- A chopping board. The cheapest and easiest to store is a plastic board.
- Some basic knives: a large serrated knife for cutting bread and cake, a medium-sized knife for chopping vegetables and cutting meat into pieces and a small knife for peeling veg and cutting up fruit.
- Everyday cutlery for eating.
- A nonstick frying pan, preferably with a lid, is invaluable for fry-ups, stir-fries and omelettes.
- A small nonstick saucepan for porridge, sauces or scrambled egg.
- A couple of bowls that stack one inside the other, for mixing salad and beating cakes.
- A couple of heavy-based saucepans with metal handles and lids for on the hob and in the oven.
- A baking sheet, roasting tin and cake tins.
- A grater with a container below means you can grate more than you need at once.
- A large sieve for draining veg, pasta or rice.
- A veg peeler, a couple of wooden spoons, a fish slice for turning fried foods, some measuring spoons, a slotted spoon, balloon whisk, a small potato masher, a tin opener and a bottle opener.
- Storage containers, a plastic lunch box for eating between studies or lectures, a couple of plastic boxes for the fridge that you can label, for storing cheese and dairy things in one, bacon in the other.
- Foil, plastic bags and clingfilm, to keep those leftovers from drying out.
- A dinner plate, tea plate and cereal bowl.
- An egg cup.

basic stores

- Tea, coffee and hot chocolate
- Onions, potatoes and garlic
- Sunflower oil
- Salt and pepper
- Vinegar, tomato ketchup
- Stock cubes
- Sugar
- Plain flour
- Breakfast cereals
- Jam or spreads
- Cans of tomatoes, baked beans, tuna
- Dried pasta, rice
- Spices – cinnamon, chilli, curry powder or separate curry spices (cumin, coriander, turmeric and garam masala)
- Dried herbs – mixed herbs, oregano and thyme
- Tomato purée, jar of pesto
- Red or green lentils, cous cous, canned or dried pulses
- Emergency jars of pasta sauce, cans of soup
- Milk, butter or spread, yogurts
- Eggs
- Bread
- Bacon or sausages
- Fruit – bananas, apples or grapes
- Fresh veg – carrots, tomatoes, cucumber, lettuce
- Fresh herbs, bunch of fresh coriander and potted basil
- Frozen peas or sweetcorn
- Frozen mixed summer fruits
- Frozen chicken pieces, minced beef, sausages, fish steaks, prawns, frozen pizza, garlic bread

Tip: If fresh herbs go a little limp, soak in cold water for an hour or so then drain and put into a sealed plastic bag and store in a drawer of the fridge. They will keep up to a week.

help...funds are low

Here are a few ideas to stretch the remaining ingredients in your store cupboard, as well as use up any fresh foods or leftovers that you have in the fridge when money is short.

baked potato toppers

Wash and scrub a medium baking potato, then prick with a fork and wrap with a sheet of kitchen paper. Place in a microwave for 6 minutes on full power or bake in a pre-heated oven 200°C (400°F), Gas Mark 6 for 1 hour or until tender. Sweet potatoes take a little less time. Slit the potato open and top with one of the following:

Baked beans spiced up with some chilli sauce

Reheated leftover Bolognese sauce sprinkled with grated Cheddar cheese. a spoonful of cream cheese or Greek yogurt, drizzled with sweet chilli sauce and some torn coriander leaves.

Canned tuna mixed with canned or frozen sweetcorn, chopped spring onions and a spoonful of mayonnaise.

Garlicky tomato sauce (see page 60) and add some sliced mushrooms and a little fresh basil.

main meal soups

These are comforting, cheap and don't require much washing up. Fry up a few diced veggies, add stock and canned beans, if you like and

simmer until the veg are tender. Serve as it is or mash if you like your soup smooth. Try flavouring the soup with chilli, garlic, fresh herbs or ground spices – for recipe ideas see Spanish Chickpea Soup on page 32 or White Bean Soup Provencal, page 28.

For another low-cost meal cook up a basic risotto and top with any vegetables you have – roasted butternut squash or cherry tomatoes, steamed broccoli or garlicky fried sliced mushrooms. Sprinkle with grated Parmesan or crumbled goats' or blue cheese. For those who prefer their rice a little spicier try the Vegetable Biriyani on page 116.

not just eggs and bacon...

If you have some potatoes, pasta, rice, beans, lentils or cous cous you have the base for as many suppers as you can think of. They're cheap, fill you up and the carbohydrate in them is complex so they are digested slowly leaving you full for longer.

Don't forget to eat fruit and veg – you need vitamin C on a daily basis. If you are low on vitamins you are more likely to go down with colds and miss out on student life! A glass of chilled orange juice is one of your five a day. Add an apple to your bag and you are on your way. Stir-fries are quick and tasty. You can use whatever you have available – some sliced carrot, broccoli or courgette, sliced chicken breast or minute steak, or a few defrosted prawns –and serve with rice or noodles. For recipe ideas see pages 174 to 177.

Egg fried rice makes another easy meal using leftover rice from the night before. First make a thin omelette in the bottom of a frying pan, slide out and roll up then fry off some chopped onion and garlic with diced bacon. Add some

mixed frozen veg and the rice, stir-fry until the veg are cooked through and the rice is hot. Flavour with soy sauce, chilli sauce or some fish sauce if you have it. Stir in the sliced omelette and warm through.

Deep dish tortillas, Spanish omelettes or frittatas are thick omelettes with lots of bits and pieces added. You can use easily available vegetables, such as onions, spring onions and mushrooms and thrown in leftovers such as sliced potatoes and sliced cooked sausage or chorizo. Omelettes are good served with a simple salad.

Hash potatoes, made with diced raw or cooked potatoes fried in oil with chopped onion and garlic can be made into a hearty supper with the addition of sliced mushrooms, diced cooked beetroot, diced bacon or ham, or even diced corned beef or canned salmon. To make bubble and squeak, add sliced cabbage or kale. To spice up the potatoes, add chilli or paprika, if you fancy. Hash potatoes can also be topped with a fried egg.

canned beans and pulses vs dried
Canned beans are indispensable, especially if cooking for one. If cooking for a crowd use cheaper dried pulses, bearing in mind that most dried pulses need to be soaked overnight. As a general guide if a recipe calls for canned beans and you would like to use dried, use half the weight of the canned beans, but remember that the can also contains water, so in a 410 g can of beans,

frying pan over a high heat for just a matter of minutes, stirring all the time for even cooking.

Shallow-fry To fry foods in a frying pan with just 1–2 tablespoons oil.

Steam To cook foods in a covered perforated saucepan set over a lower saucepan half-filled with boiling water, so it is not in direct contact with water.

Simmer Cook over a low heat so the bubbles break the surface.

Mash This can be done with a fork, for example, when mashing a banana or avocado on a plate until smooth. Larger amounts of vegetables are best mashed with a larger metal masher or hand held-stick blender.

Roux This is the base of a cheese or white sauce. To make a roux, melt the butter in a saucepan, then stir in the flour until the mixture binds together. Cook briefly, then stir in milk with a wooden spoon until smooth. Continue to stir until the sauce comes to the boil, is a pouring thickness and hopefully lump free. If there are lumps in your sauce, these can be whisked out with a small balloon whisk.

Rubbing in This odd sounding term is used when making shortcrust pastry and in some cakes. Butter is cut into small cubes and added to flour. Dip your hands into this mixture and lift it up, then quite literally rub the mixture between your fingertips to break up the fat until it looks like fine breadcrumbs.

Creaming This term is used when making cakes. Butter or soft margarine is beaten with sugar in a bowl with a wooden spoon or electric mixer, if you have one, until it is creamy smooth and pale in colour.

the drained weight of beans is 235g.

Red, green and the tiny Puy lentils don't need soaking overnight before you cook them, and couscous only needs only soaking in boiling water for 5 minutes before use.

Adding beans, lentils or root vegetables to meaty casseroles means you can cut down the amount of meat per serving without compromising on portion size.

Breakfast cereals needn't only be eaten for breakfast, they're low in fat and served with milk make a quick healthy anytime-of-day snack. Top with some sliced bananas, some diced dried apricots, or a few raisins or a few fresh berries, if you have them.

crash course in cooking terms...

Stir-fry To cook thinly sliced vegetables and meat or fish in a little oil in a wok or large

get used to your oven

All ovens vary slightly. Fan ovens cook more quickly than those with top and bottom heat. As a general rule, for a fan oven use an oven temperature 10–20° below the temperatures given in the recipes in this book and check on food in the oven 10–15 minutes before the end of cooking to make sure it isn't overcooking. If the food is overbrowning cover the top with foil to stop it burning and lower the oven temperature slightly.

how can you tell if food is cooked?

Chicken, turkey and pork must be thoroughly cooked before serving. Even though recipes have cooking times it is always worth double-checking food is cooked through before you serve it up. To test whether meat and poultry is cooked, insert a skewer or thin bladed knife into the thickest part of the meat. For a whole chicken or turkey, skewer through the thickest part of the drumstick into the breast meat, then wait for a few seconds – if the juices run clear it is ready, if there are any traces of pink, indicating blood is still present then it needs a little longer. Cook for 10 minutes more then test again. For pork chops or a joint insert the skewer into the centre then check the meat juices in the same way.

Beef and lamb can be eaten slightly pink, according to taste.

Fish is cooked through when it is the same colour all the way through and the flesh breaks easily into flakes. Uncooked prawns

will turn pink all over when cooked through. Fresh tuna is the only exception and like beef steak can be eaten 'rare'.

When cooked, pasta and rice should be tender with a little bite – for pasta this is called al dente. To check, take a little out of the pan, cool, then taste. The same goes for vegetables – take a small piece out the pan and eat when cool enough, but remember that the large pieces will take longer to cook, so test these with a knife: if it goes in easily they are tender.

To check if a cake is cooked, don't open the oven for the first 20 minutes or the cake will sink; check at regular intervals after this time so it doesn't burn. Press the top of a shallow sandwich-style cake with your fingertip; if it feels firm or springs back then it is ready. For deeper cakes, press a wooden skewer or small knife into the centre; if it comes out clean the cake is ready, if it is smeared with mixture cook a little longer and then check again. Cover the top of the cake with foil if it seems to be browning too quickly.

improvising

Don't have a rolling pin? Try using a washed beer glass or cordial bottle, or even a washed full can of fizzy drink.

Need a biscuit cutter? Use an upturned, clean glass and cut around the rim with a small knife.

To make breadcrumbs without a food processor, grate the crust, bread or bread roll on the coarse section of a grater. The bread needs to be in one chunk, sliced bread will mean fingers get grated too.

Want to steam some veg but don't have a special steamer pan, then put the veg into a large metal sieve or colander and set this over a saucepan half-filled with boiling water making sure that the water is well below the sieve or colander. Cover with a large lid and cook until the veg are just tender.

Short of pans or oven space? Rice noodles don't need cooking in the same way as wheat pasta but can be soaked in a bowl of boiling water for 3–5 minutes until soft and hot, then drained and added to stir-fries

Don't have quite the right pan? Use what you do have – metal saucepans with metal handles can be used on the hob and in the oven: china or pottery casserole dishes can only be used in the oven, so fry off meat and veggies in a frying pan, add the stock and

bring to the boil then transfer to the casserole and finish off in the oven.

Cake tin is bigger than you need? Reduce the recipe cooking time as the cake will be thinner and therefore cook more quickly. Increase the cooking time if the tin is smaller than required, as the cake will be deeper and so take longer to cook. To check if the cake is cooked see opposite.

Don't have any scales or a measuring jug? Use spoons, cups and glasses. 1 level tablespoon measuring spoon = 15 g (½ oz), 1 tablespoon = 3 teaspoons. 1 teacup = 250ml (8fl oz). 1 pint beer glass = 600 ml.

do s and don ts

• Metal things can't be used in a microwave. This includes metallic trims on glass or china.

• Keep dairy and meat items separately, and raw and cooked meat apart in the fridge. Make sure food is covered so it doesn't dry out.

• Check dates on bought food, sell by dates are the dates food must be sold by in the shops, use by dates, the date it must be eaten by at home. Throw food away after that date.

• Cook frozen veggies and fruit from frozen.

• Meat and fish must be defrosted thoroughly before cooking.

• Do not put defrosted food back in the freezer.

• To speed up defrosting, put frozen food in cold water NOT HOT, and change the water several times.

• Only reheat food once and make sure that the food is boiling hot right through to the centre. If you only need one portion reheated take it out of a larger dish and put the rest back into the fridge.

soups,
stews &
casseroles

pork & red pepper chilli

Serves **4**
Preparation time **10 minutes**
Cooking time **30 minutes**

2 tablespoons **olive oil**
1 large **onion**, chopped
1 **red pepper**, cored,
   deseeded and diced
2 **garlic cloves**, crushed
450 g (14½ oz) **minced pork**
1 **fresh red chilli**, deseeded
   and finely chopped
1 teaspoon **dried oregano**
500 g (1 lb) **passata** (sieved
   tomatoes)
400 g (13 oz) can **red kidney
   beans,** drained and rinsed
salt and **pepper**
basil leaves, to garnish
soured cream, to serve

Heat the oil in a saucepan over a medium heat. Add the onion and red pepper and cook for 5 minutes until soft and starting to brown, then add the garlic and cook for another 30 seconds or so. Next, add the minced pork and cook, stirring and breaking up the meat with a wooden spoon, for 5 minutes or until browned.

Add the remaining ingredients, except the soured cream, and bring to the boil. Reduce the heat and simmer gently for 20 minutes. Remove from the heat, season well with salt and pepper and garnish with soured cream and basil leaves. Serve with boiled rice or crusty bread on the side.

For lamb & aubergine chilli, replace the red pepper with 1 medium aubergine, cut into small cubes. Fry as above with the onion and garlic, then add 450 g (14½ oz) minced lamb instead of the pork. Continue as above. Sprinkle the finished dish with 2 tablespoons finely chopped mint leaves, omitting the soured cream, and serve with rice or pasta.

vietnamese beef pho

Serves **6**
Preparation time **15 minutes**
Cooking time **20 minutes**

1.5 litres (2½ pints) good-
   quality **chicken stock**
2 **lemon grass stalks**, bruised
small piece of **fresh root
   ginger**, peeled and
   thinly sliced
2 tablespoons **light soy sauce**
2 tablespoons **lime juice**
2 teaspoons **soft dark brown
   sugar**
125 g (4 oz) **dried flat rice
   noodles**
275 g (9 oz) **sirloin steak**,
   sliced

To serve
150 g (5 oz) **bean sprouts**
1 **fresh red chilli**, deseeded
   and thinly sliced
handful of **Thai basil**
handful of **mint**

Put the stock, lemon grass, ginger, soy sauce, lime juice and sugar in a large heavy-based saucepan and bring to the boil. Reduce the heat and simmer gently for 10 minutes until fragrant.

Remove the lemon grass and ginger using a slotted spoon; discard. Add the rice noodles to the simmering broth and cook according to the packet instructions, adding the sliced steak for the last 2–3 minutes of the cooking time to cook through.

Spoon into warm soup bowls, top with the bean sprouts, chilli, basil and mint and serve immediately.

For salmon pho, cook the stock using fish stock insteaad of chicken stock. Dice 250 g (8 oz) skinned and pin-boned salmon (or trout) fillets, add to the fragrant stock after removing the lemon grass and ginger and simmer for 6–8 minutes until the fish is just cooked through. Meanwhile, cook the rice noodles separately in boiling water for 2–3 minutes. Drain and divide among 6 warm soup bowls, then spoon over the broth. Top with the bean sprouts, chilli and herbs, and serve immediately.

gruyère, bacon & potato soup

Serves **6**
Preparation time **20 minutes**
Cooking time **30 minutes**

2 tablespoons **olive oil**
3 **rindless smoked bacon
rashers**, chopped
2 **onions**, finely chopped
600 ml (1 pint) good-quality
chicken stock
900 ml (1½ pints) **water**
625 g (1¼ lb) **potatoes**,
peeled and cut into 1 cm
(½ inch) cubes
4 tablespoons **plain flour**
50 g (2 oz) **Gruyère cheese**,
grated
1 tablespoon **medium-dry
sherry**
1 teaspoon **Worcestershire
sauce**
3 tablespoons finely chopped
flat leaf parsley (optional)
salt and **pepper**

Put the oil in a large heavy-based saucepan over a medium heat. Add the bacon and onions and cook for about 5 minutes until the onion is soft and pale golden.

Pour in the stock and 600 ml (1 pint) of the measurement water, add the potatoes and bring to the boil. Reduce the heat, cover and simmer for about 15 minutes until the potatoes are tender.

Whisk the flour with the remaining measurement water in a small bowl then stir the mixture into the soup. Cover and simmer, stirring frequently, for another 5 minutes.

Blend the Gruyère with 300 ml (½ pint) of the soup in a blender or food processor until smooth. Return to the pan and add the sherry and Worcestershire sauce. Season with salt and pepper, bearing in mind the saltiness of the bacon and cheese. Gently simmer for 3–5 minutes.

Stir in the parsley, if using, and serve immediately in warm soup bowls with grilled cheese on toast sprinkled with a little Worcestershire sauce, if liked.

For celeriac soup with bacon & blue cheese, fry the bacon and onions in the oil as above. Add the stock, measurement water and 625 g (1¼ lb) peeled and diced celeriac instead of the potatoes. Continue as above, adding 50 g (2 oz) blue cheese such as Stilton or Danish blue, rind removed and diced, instead of the Gruyère. Purée the soup until smooth, then return to the pan to heat through, omitting the sherry and Worcestershire sauce. Garnish with the parsley and some extra diced cheese.

jamaican pepperpot soup

Serves **6**
Preparation time **20 minutes**
Cooking time **1 hour**
10 minutes

1 kg (2 lb) **lean stewing beef**,
  cut into cubes
250 g (8 oz) **boneless lean
  pork**, cut into cubes
2.5 litres (4 pints) **water**
24 **okra**, trimmed and
  chopped
500 g (1 lb) **kale**, tough stalks
  discarded, roughly chopped
2 **green peppers**, cored,
  deseeded and chopped
2 **spring onions**, roughly
  chopped
sprig of **thyme**
¼ teaspoon **cayenne pepper**
500 g (1 lb) **yellow yams**,
  peeled and diced
2 small **potatoes**, peeled and
  sliced
1 **garlic clove**, finely chopped
salt

Put the meat and measurement water in a large
saucepan. Bring to the boil, then reduce the heat,
partially cover and simmer for about 30 minutes.

Add the okra, kale, green peppers and spring onions to
the soup with the thyme and cayenne pepper. Partially
cover and simmer over a medium heat for 15 minutes.

Tip in the yams, potatoes and garlic and simmer for
another 20 minutes or until the yams and potato are
tender and the meat is cooked through. Add more
water if the soup is too thick. Season with salt and
serve in warm soup bowls with crusty bread, if liked.

For extra hot pepperpot soup with dumplings,

add a 7 cm (3 inch) piece of fresh root ginger, finely
chopped, and 2 deseeded and finely chopped Scotch
bonnet chillies instead of the cayenne pepper. While
the yams cook, mix 150 g (5 oz) plain flour with a little
salt and 4–5 tablespoons water to make the dumpling
dough; it should be soft and slightly sticky. Rub your
hands with a little vegetable oil, then divide the dough
into 24 pieces, shape into ovals and carefully drop the
dumplings into the soup. Cover the pan again and cook
for about 10 minutes.

meat tortellini in brodo

Serves **4**
Preparation time **5 minutes**
Cooking time **20 minutes**

8 sheets **fresh lasagne sheets**
semola di grano duro
   (coarse semolina) for dusting
600 ml (1 pint) good quality
   beef or chicken
   stock, boiling
2 **tomatoes**, diced
handful of **basil leaves**
salt and **pepper**
freshly grated **Parmesan**
   cheese, to serve

Filling
1 teaspoon **olive oil**
1 small **onion**, finely chopped
1 **garlic clove**, finely chopped
200 g (7 oz) **minced pork**
50 g (2 oz) **prosciutto crudo**,
   roughly chopped
1 tablespoon chopped **flat leaf**
   parsley
4 tablespoons **dry white wine**
2 tablespoons freshly grated
   Parmesan cheese
2 tablespoons **dried**
   breadcrumbs
¼ teaspoon freshly grated
   nutmeg

Make the filling first. Heat the oil in a heavy-based frying pan over a low heat. Add the onion and garlic. Cook, stirring frequently, for 6–7 minutes until soft and translucent. Add the meat and prosciutto, and cook over a medium heat, breaking up and stirring frequently, for 10 minutes until the meat is cooked. Add the parsley and wine and cook until the liquid has evaporated. Cool and transfer to a food processor or blender with the remaining filling ingredients. Season and blend to a coarse paste.

Cut the lasagne sheets into 8 cm (3½ inch) squares and place a nutmeg-sized ball of filling in the centre of each square. Brush a little water around the edges of the squares, then fold the dough over the filling to make triangles. Gently but firmly push down around the filling, sealing the pasta and ensuring that no air has been trapped. Bring the corners on the longest edge of the triangles together, and pinch tightly to seal. Set aside on a baking sheet lightly dusted with semola di grano duro, and cover with a clean tea towel.

Put the stock in a large saucepan, and season with a little salt. Add the tortellini, diced tomatoes and basil, and cook for 2–3 minutes until al dente. Serve the tortellini in warm bowls with the broth, and grated Parmesan.

For speedy spinach tortellini in brodo, heat 1 litre (1¾ pints) good-quality chicken stock in a large saucepan. Add 2 x 300 g (10 oz) packets ready-made chilled spinach-stuffed tortellini. Cook as above, omitting the tomatoes and basil. Add 150 g (5 oz) fresh spinach and 2 tablespoons lemon juice, season with salt and pepper, and cook for another 1 minute until the spinach just wilts. Serve with freshly grated Parmesan cheese.

white bean soup provençal

Serves **6**

Preparation time **15 minutes**,
   plus soaking

Cooking time **1¼–1¾ hours**

3 tablespoons **olive oil**

2 **garlic cloves**, crushed

1 small **red pepper**, cored,
   deseeded and chopped

1 **onion**, finely chopped

250 g (8 oz) **tomatoes**, finely
   chopped

1 teaspoon finely chopped
   thyme

400 g (14 oz) can **dried
   haricot** or **cannellini beans**,
   soaked overnight in cold
   water, rinsed and drained

600 ml (1 pint) **water**

600 ml (1 pint) **vegetable
   stock**

2 tablespoons finely chopped
   flat leaf parsley

salt and **pepper**

Heat the oil in a large heavy-based saucepan, add the garlic, red pepper and onion and cook over a medium heat for 5 minutes or until softened.

Add the tomatoes and thyme and cook for 1 minute. Add the beans and pour in the measurement water and stock. Bring to the boil, then reduce the heat, cover and simmer for 1–1½ hours until the beans are tender (you may need to allow for a longer cooking time, depending on how old the beans are).

Sprinkle in the parsley and season with salt and pepper. Serve immediately in warm soup bowls with fresh, crusty bread.

For Spanish white bean soup, add 100 g (3½ oz) diced chorizo sausage when frying the onions, garlic and red pepper. Stir in 1 teaspoon pimentón (Spanish smoked paprika) or 1 teaspoon mild chilli powder. Cook for 1 minute until fragrant, then add the tomatoes and continue the recipe as above.

quick sausage & bean casserole

Serves **4**
Preparation time **5 minutes**
Cooking time **25 minutes**

2 tablespoons **olive oil**
16 **cocktail sausages**,
  separated
2 **garlic cloves**, crushed
400 g (13 oz) can **chopped
  tomatoes**
400 g (13 oz) can **baked
  beans**
200 g (7 oz) can **mixed
  beans**, drained and rinsed
½ teaspoon **dried thyme**
salt and **pepper**
3 tablespoons chopped **flat
  leaf parsley** (optional),
  to garnish

Heat the oil in a frying pan over a medium-high heat.
Add the sausages and cook for a few minutes until
nicely browned all over.

Transfer the sausages to a large saucepan and add the
remaining ingredients except the parsley. Bring to the
boil, then reduce the heat, cover tightly and simmer for
20 minutes until the sausages are cooked through.

Season with salt and pepper, sprinkle with the parsley,
if using, and serve hot with mustard mash (see below).

For mustard mash, to serve as an accompaniment,
cook 1 kg (2 lb) chopped floury potatoes in a large
saucepan of salted boiling water until tender; be
careful not to overcook, or the potatoes will become
waterlogged. Drain well and return to the pan. Mash
with 75 g (3 oz) butter, 1 tablespoon wholegrain
mustard, 3 teaspoons prepared English mustard and
1 crushed garlic clove. Season with salt and pepper,
then beat in 2 tablespoons chopped flat leaf parsley
and a dash of olive oil. Serve hot with the casserole.

spanish chickpea soup

Serves **8**
Preparation time **15 minutes**,
  plus soaking
Cooking time **2¼ hours**

150 g (5 oz) **dried chickpeas**,
  soaked for 48 hours in
  cold water or 12 hours in
  boiling water
500–750 g (1–1½ lb)
  **boneless smoked bacon
  hock joint**
1 **onion**, studded with
  4 **cloves**
2 **garlic cloves,** crushed
1 **bay leaf**
sprig of **thyme**
sprig of **marjoram**
sprig of **flat leaf parsley**
1.8 litres (3 pints) **water**
1.8 litres (3 pints) **chicken
  stock**
300–375 g (10–12 oz)
  potatoes, cut into 1 cm
  (½ inch) cubes
300 g (10 oz) **Savoy
  cabbage**, shredded
salt and **pepper**

Drain the chickpeas, rinse under cold running water
and drain again. Put the bacon joint in a large, deep
saucepan and cover with cold water. Bring the water
briefly to the boil, then drain, discarding the water.

Transfer the bacon joint to a clean, large heavy-based
saucepan. Add the chickpeas, studded onion, garlic, bay
leaf, thyme, marjoram, parsley and measurement water.
Bring to the boil, then reduce the heat, partially cover
and simmer for 1½ hours until the meat is tender.

Remove and discard the onion and herbs. Remove the
hock, transfer to a board and cut into small pieces. Set
aside. Add the stock, potatoes and cabbage to the pan,
and simmer for a further 30 minutes.

Add the reserved hock pieces to the soup and cook
for a further 10 minutes. Season with salt and pepper.
Ladle the soup into warm soup bowls and serve with
fresh, crusty bread.

For mixed pea & bacon soup, replace the chickpeas
with 150 g (5 oz) country soup mix (a blend of dried
yellow and green split peas, pearl barley and red lentils).
Put the country soup mix in a sieve, pick over for any
grit or damaged lentils and rinse under cold running
water. Drain and add to the pan with the bacon joint;
bring to the boil, then drain. Transfer to a clean pan and
add the clove-studded onion, 2 bay leaves, 2 teaspoons
prepared English mustard and the measurement water.
Continue as above. Add the stock, potatoes and 2 diced
carrots, omitting the cabbage. Finish the soup as above.

noodle soup with prawn tempura

Serves **5**
Preparation time **20 minutes**
Cooking time **15 minutes**

125 g (4 oz) **dried soba noodles**
2 teaspoons **sesame oil**
1 bunch of **spring onions**, sliced
2 **pak choi**, shredded
1.8 litres (3 pints) **hot vegetable stock**
4 tablespoons **sake**
2 tablespoons **dark soy sauce**
125 g (4 oz) **bean sprouts**
vegetable oil, for deep-frying
12 **raw tiger prawns**, thawed if frozen, peeled and deveined
2 sheets of **nori**, shredded (optional)

Tempura batter
1 **egg yolk**
50 g (2 oz) **plain flour**
100 ml (3½ fl oz) **iced water**

Cook the soba noodles according to the packet instructions. Rinse in a colander under hot running water. Drain well.

Heat the sesame oil in a large wok. Add the spring onions and pak choi, and stir-fry over medium-high heat for 1 minute. Pour in the stock, sake and soy sauce and simmer gently for 5 minutes. Stir in the bean sprouts.

Make the tempura while the stir-fry is simmering. In a bowl, briefly whisk together the egg yolk, flour and water to make a slightly lumpy batter. Heat the vegetable oil in a separate wok, a deep heavy-based saucepan or a deep-fat fryer to 180°–190°C (350°–375°F), or until a cube of bread dropped into the oil browns in 30 seconds. Dip the prawns in the batter, then carefully drop them into the hot oil and cook for 3 minutes or until the prawns have turned pink and the batter is golden. Remove with a slotted spoon and drain on kitchen paper.

Spoon the noodles into warm soup bowls, add the soup and top with the prawns and strips of nori, if liked. Serve immediately.

For noodle soup with black beans, make up the noodles and soup as above, but omit the prawn tempura. Add 125 ml (4 fl oz) black bean sauce or stir-fry sauce and ½–1 deseeded and sliced small fresh red chilli with the stock, sake and soy sauce. Simmer the soup for 5 minutes, then add the bean sprouts. Serve immediately, sprinkled with chopped peanuts instead of the prawns and nori topping.

goulash soup

Serves **6**
Preparation time **15 minutes**
Cooking time 1 ¼ **hours**

3 tablespoons **vegetable oil**
750 g (1 ½ lb) **boneless
    lean beef**, cut into 2.5 cm
    (1 inch) strips
2 **onions**, chopped
2 **garlic cloves**, crushed
2 **celery sticks**, sliced
3 tablespoons **paprika**
1 tablespoon **caraway seeds**
1.2 litres (2 pints) **beef stock**
600 ml (1 pint) **water**
¼ teaspoon **dried thyme**
2 bay leaves
¼ teaspoon **Tabasco sauce**
    (or to taste)
3 tablespoons **tomato purée**
250 g (8 oz) **potatoes**,
    peeled and cut into 1 cm
    (½ inch) cubes
3 **carrots**, cut into 1 cm
    (½ inch) cubes
soured cream, to serve
    (optional)

Put the oil in a large heavy-based saucepan over a medium-high heat. When the oil is hot, add the beef, in batches to avoid crowding the pan, and cook for a few minutes until browned all over. As each batch browns, remove with a slotted spoon and drain on kitchen paper. Reduce the heat to medium and add the onions, garlic and celery to the pan. Cook for 5 minutes or until softened.

Remove from the heat and stir in the paprika and caraway seeds. Pour in the stock and measurement water. Add the thyme, bay leaves, Tabasco sauce and tomato purée. Stir well and add the browned beef. Bring to the boil, then reduce the heat, partially cover and simmer for about 30 minutes.

Add the potatoes and carrots and simmer for another 30 minutes or until the beef and potatoes are tender. Remove and discard the bay leaves. Spoon the soup into warm soup bowls, garnish each portion with a dollop of soured cream, if liked, and serve immediately.

For goulash soup with white fish, make up the soup as above, omitting the beef and using 1.2 litres (2 pints) fish stock instead of the beef stock and measurement water. Simmer for 30 minutes, then add 500 g (1 lb) skinned haddock or cod fillet. Simmer gently for another 10 minutes, then lift out the fish and break into pieces. Remove any bones, then return the fish to the soup. Serve with soured cream, sprinkled with a little chopped dill or flat leaf parsley.

chicken stew with dumplings

Serves **4**
Preparation time **30 minutes**
Cooking time 1½ **hours**

8 **boneless, skinless chicken
    thighs**, halved
1 tablespoon **sunflower oil**
1 **onion**, roughly chopped
2 **parsnips**, cut into chunks
2 **carrots**, cut into chunks
175 g (6 oz) **swede**, cut into
    chunks
50 g (2 oz) **pearl barley**
350 ml (12 fl oz) bottle
    pale ale
300 ml (½ pint) **chicken stock**
2 teaspoons **prepared
    English mustard**
salt and **pepper**

Dumplings
175 g (6 oz) **self-raising flour**
75 g (3 oz) **light shredded
    suet**
4 tablespoons chopped
    chives
100–125 ml (3½–4 fl oz)
    cold water

Put the oil in a flameproof casserole over a high heat.
When the oil is hot, add the chicken and onion, and fry
for about 5 minutes until golden.

Stir in the remaining vegetables and cook for
2 minutes until starting to soften, then mix in the pearl
barley, ale, stock and mustard. Season with salt and
pepper and bring to the boil. Cover and transfer to a
preheated oven, 180°C (350°F), Gas Mark 4, for 1 hour.

Make the dumplings almost at the end of the chicken
stew's cooking time. Mix together the flour, suet and
chives in a bowl and season with a little salt and pepper.
Stir in enough of the measurement water, adding a little
at a time, to mix to a soft, slightly sticky dough. Shape
dessertspoons of the mixture into balls.

Remove the chicken stew from the oven, transfer to
the hob and stir through. When the stock is boiling,
carefully add the dumplings so that they sit on the
surface, leaving space around each one. Cover and
simmer for about 15 minutes until the dumplings are
light and fluffy and the chicken is cooked through.
(Keeping the lid on while cooking makes the dumplings
rise well). Spoon into warm shallow bowls to serve.

For chicken hotpot, omit the dumplings and cover
the top of the stew with 625 g (1¼ lb) peeled and
thinly sliced potatoes arranged in an overlapping layer
before it goes into the oven. Cover and cook for 1 hour.
Remove the lid, dot the potatoes with 25 g (1 oz) butter,
season with salt and pepper and cook for another
30 minutes until the potatoes are lightly browned and
the chicken is cooked through.

spiced lamb & sweet potato soup

Serves **6**
Preparation time **30 minutes**
Cooking time **2¾–3 hours**

1 tablespoon **olive oil**
500 g (1 lb) **stewing lamb on the bone**
1 **onion**, finely chopped
1–2 **garlic cloves**, finely chopped
2.5 cm (1 inch) piece of **fresh root ginger**, grated
2 teaspoons **ras el hanout** (Moroccan spice blend)
2 litres (3½ pints) **lamb** or **chicken stock**
75 g (3 oz) **red lentils**, picked over, rinsed and drained
300 g (10 oz) **sweet potatoes**, peeled and diced
175 g (6 oz) **carrots**, diced
salt and **pepper**
small bunch of **fresh coriander**, to garnish (optional)

Heat the oil in a large heavy-based saucepan over a medium-high heat. When the oil is hot, add the lamb and fry for a couple of minutes until browned on one side. Reduce the heat slightly, turn the meat over and add the onion. Continue cooking until the lamb is browned all over and the onion is softened and starting to colour.

Stir in the garlic, ginger and ras el hanout. Cook, stirring, for about 30 seconds until fragrant, then add the stock and lentils. Season with salt and pepper. Bring to the boil, reduce the heat, cover and simmer for 1½ hours.

Add the sweet potatoes and carrots, bring back to a simmer, then cover the pan again and simmer the soup gently for 1 hour. Lift the lamb out of the soup with a slotted spoon, transfer to a plate and carefully remove the bones and any excess fat, breaking the meat into small pieces. Return the meat to the pan and heat through. Taste and adjust the seasoning if liked. Ladle the soup into bowls, sprinkle with torn coriander leaves and serve with hot flat breads.

For homemade fennel flat breads, to serve as an accompaniment, put 200 g (7 oz) self-raising flour and ½ teaspoon baking powder in a bowl. Using a mortar and pestle, crush 1 teaspoon fennel seeds. Add the crushed seeds to the flour and season with salt and pepper. Stir. Add 2 tablespoons olive oil, then gradually mix in 100 ml (3½ fl oz) water, a little at a time, using just enough to make a soft dough. Cut the dough into 6 pieces, then roll out each piece on a lightly floured surface into a rough oval shape about the size of a hand. Cook on a preheated griddle pan or heavy frying pan for 3–4 minutes each side until singed and puffy.

quick one-pot ratatouille

Serves **4**

Preparation time **10 minutes**

Cooking time **20 minutes**

100 ml (3½ fl oz) **olive oil**

2 **onions**, chopped

1 **aubergine**, cut into bite-sized cubes

2 large **courgettes**, cut into bite-sized pieces

1 **red pepper**, cored, deseeded and cut into bite-sized pieces

1 **yellow pepper**, cored, deseeded and cut into bite-sized pieces

2 **garlic cloves**, crushed

400 g (13 oz) can **chopped tomatoes**

4 tablespoons chopped **parsley** or **basil**

salt and **pepper**

Heat the oil in a large saucepan until very hot. Add the onions, aubergine, courgettes, red and yellow peppers and garlic, and cook, stirring constantly, for a few minutes until softened. Add the tomatoes, season with salt and pepper and stir well.

Reduce the heat, cover the pan tightly and simmer for 15 minutes until all the vegetables are cooked. Remove from the heat and stir in the chopped parsley or basil before serving.

For Mediterranean vegetable pie, spoon the cooked vegetable mixture into a medium-sized ovenproof dish. Cook 800 g (1 lb 10 oz) peeled and quartered floury potatoes in a large saucepan of salted boiling water for 12–15 minutes until tender. Drain and roughly mash with 200 g (7 oz) finely grated Cheddar cheese. Spread over the vegetable mixture, then bake in a preheated oven, 180°C (350°F), Gas Mark 4, for 20 minutes or until lightly golden on top.

steak & ale casserole

Serves **5–6**
Preparation time **20 minutes**
Cooking time **1¾ hours**

2 tablespoons **plain flour**
1 kg (2 lb) **braising steak**,
　cut into chunks
25 g (1 oz) **butter**
1 tablespoon **vegetable oil**
2 **onions**, chopped
2 **celery sticks**, sliced
a few **sprigs** of **thyme**
2 **bay leaves**
400 ml (14 fl oz) **strong ale**
300 ml (½ pint) **beef stock**
2 tablespoons **black treacle**
500 g (1 lb) **parsnips**, peeled
　and cut into wedges
salt and **pepper**

Season the flour with salt and pepper and use to coat the beef. Melt the butter with the oil in a large flameproof casserole over a medium-high heat. Working in batches to avoid crowding the casserole, fry the beef for a few minutes until well browned all over. As each batch browns, remove with a slotted spoon and set aside on a plate.

Put the onions and celery in the casserole and fry gently for 5 minutes until soft and translucent. Return the beef to the pan and add the herbs, ale, stock and treacle. Stir through. Bring just to the boil, then reduce the heat and cover. Bake in a preheated oven, 160°C (325°F), Gas Mark 3, for 1 hour.

Add the parsnips to the casserole, cover again and return to the oven for another 30 minutes or until the beef and parsnips are tender. Check the seasoning and serve.

For Irish champ, to serve as an accompaniment, cook 1.5 kg (3 lb) scrubbed floury potatoes in a large saucepan of salted boiling water for 20 minutes. Peel away the skins, then return to the pan and mash. Beat in 150 ml (¼ pint) milk, 3–4 finely chopped spring onions and 50 g (2 oz) butter. Season with salt and pepper. Serve hot.

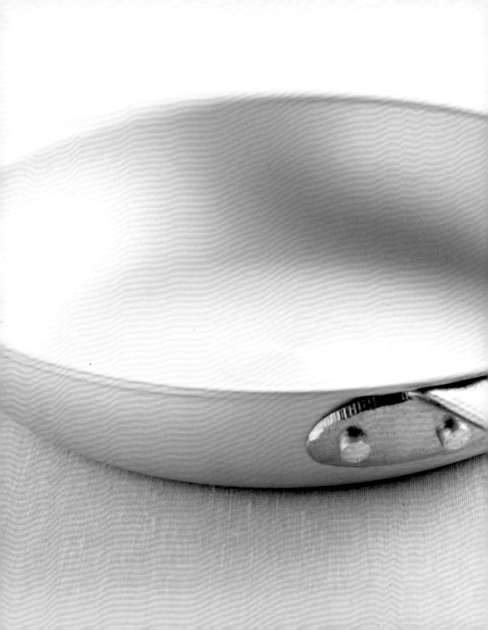

simple
suppers

pasta with tomato & basil sauce

Serves **4**

Preparation time **10 minutes**

Cooking time **10 minutes**

400 g (13 oz) **dried spaghetti**
75 ml (3 fl oz) **olive oil**
5 **garlic cloves**, finely chopped
6 **vine-ripened tomatoes**,
  deseeded and chopped
25 g (1 oz) **basil leaves**
salt and **pepper**

Cook the pasta in a large saucepan of salted boiling water according to the packet instructions until al dente.

Heat half the oil while the pasta is cooking in a frying pan over a low heat. Add the garlic and cook for 1 minute. As soon as the garlic begins to change colour, remove the pan from the heat and add the remaining oil.

Drain the pasta and return to the pan. Add the garlic-infused oil with the chopped tomatoes and basil leaves. Season and toss well to mix. Serve immediately.

For quick tomato & basil pizza, prepare the garlic-infused oil as above, but use 4 tablespoons olive oil and 4 finely chopped garlic cloves. Meanwhile, skin the tomatoes and deseed and chop as above. Pour off half the oil and reserve, add the tomatoes and half the basil to the pan, season well with salt and pepper and leave to simmer while you make the dough. Sift 250 g (8 oz) self-raising flour and 1 teaspoon salt into a large bowl, then gradually add 150 ml (¼ pint) warm water, mixing well to form a soft dough. Work the dough into a ball with your hands. Knead on a lightly floured surface until smooth and soft. Roll out the dough to a 30 cm (12 inch) round, making a border around the edge slightly thicker than the centre, and lay on a warmed baking sheet. Spread the tomato mixture over the dough base, top with 125 g (4 oz) sliced mozzarella cheese and drizzle with the remaining garlic oil. Bake in a preheated oven, 240°C (475°F), Gas Mark 9, for 15 minutes or until the base is golden. Scatter with the remaining basil leaves and serve immediately.

thai sesame chicken patties

Serves **4**

Preparation time **15 minutes**,
   plus chilling

Cooking time **10 minutes**

4 **spring onions**

15 g (½ oz) **fresh coriander**,
   plus extra to garnish

500 g (1 lb) **minced chicken**

3 tablespoons **sesame seeds**,
   toasted

1 tablespoon **light soy sauce**

3.5 cm (1½ inch) piece of
   fresh root ginger, peeled
   and finely grated

1 **egg white**

1 tablespoon **sesame oil**

1 tablespoon **sunflower oil**

**Thai sweet chilli dipping
   sauce**, to serve

spring onion curls, to garnish
   (optional)

Chop the spring onions and coriander finely in a food processor or with a knife. Put in a bowl and mix with the chicken, sesame seeds, soy sauce, ginger and egg white.

Divide the mixture into 20 mounds on a chopping board, then shape into slightly flattened rounds with wetted hands. Chill in the refrigerator for 1 hour (or longer if you have time).

Heat the sesame and sunflower oils in a large frying pan, add the patties and fry for 10 minutes, turning once or twice, until golden and cooked through to the centre.

Arrange on a serving plate with a small bowl of chilli dipping sauce in the centre. Garnish with extra coriander leaves and spring onion curls, if liked.

For baby leaf stir-fry with chilli, to serve as an accompaniment, heat 2 teaspoons sesame oil in the same pan used to cook the patties. Add a 250 g (8 oz) pack of ready-prepared baby leaf and baby vegetable stir-fry ingredients and stir-fry for 2–3 minutes until the vegetables are hot. Mix in 2 tablespoons light soy sauce and 1 tablespoon Thai sweet chilli dipping sauce. Serve in a side bowl with the chicken patties.

cod with roasted tomato toast

Serves **4**
Preparation time **15 minutes**
Cooking time 1 ¼ **hours**

4 ripe **tomatoes**, halved
a few sprigs of **thyme**
2 tablespoons **olive oil**
4 **cod fillets**, about 200 g
   (7 oz) each, skin on and
   pin-boned
4 slices of **ciabatta**
1 **garlic clove**
salt and **pepper**
Parmesan cheese shavings,
   to garnish (optional)

Dressing
large handful of **basil**
4 tablespoons **olive oil**
2 tablespoons freshly grated
   Parmesan cheese

Arrange the tomato halves on a baking sheet, season with salt and pepper, sprinkle with the thyme and drizzle with 1 tablespoon of the oil. Roast in a preheated oven, 160°C (325°F), Gas Mark 3, for 1 hour until soft, then increase the oven temperature to 180°C (350°F), Gas Mark 4.

Season the cod, towards the end of the tomatoes' cooking time, and roast the cod along with the tomatoes in the oven for 10–12 minutes until the fish is cooked and the tomatoes have softened.

Brush both sides of the bread with the remaining oil. Preheat a ridged griddle pan and griddle the bread until golden brown on both sides. Then rub both sides with the garlic clove.

Put the ingredients for the dressing in a small food processor and blend until smooth. You can also do this using a hand-held blender.

Top the toast with the tomatoes, then serve with the cod. Drizzle a little of the dressing over the top and garnish with some Parmesan shavings, if liked.

For roasted cod & tomato pasta, while the tomatoes and cod are roasting as above, cook 300 g (10 oz) dried pasta according to the packet instructions until al dente, then drain. Cut the roasted tomatoes into small pieces and flake the cod. Stir through the warm pasta with some of the dressing, prepared as above.

indonesian-style curry

Serves **4–6**
Preparation time **30 minutes**
Cooking time **4½ hours**

3 tablespoons **coconut** or
   vegetable oil
750 g (1½ lb) **braising beef**, sliced
800 ml (26 fl oz) **coconut milk**
250 ml (8 fl oz) **water**
1 tablespoon **palm sugar** or **soft
   brown sugar**
4 **kaffir lime leaves**, shredded
3 **star anise**
1 large **cinnamon stick**
½ teaspoon **salt**

Spice paste

1 teaspoon **salt**, **ground turmeric**
½ teaspoon **chilli powder**
6 **garlic cloves**, chopped
5 cm (2 inch) piece of **fresh root
   ginger**, peeled and grated
5 cm (2 inch) piece of **fresh
   galangal**, peeled and grated
1 teaspoon **black peppercorns**,
   crushed
4 **cardamom pods**, bruised
4 **fresh red chillies**, chopped
1 **lemon grass stalk**, tough outer
   layers removed, chopped
3 large **onions**, chopped
1 tablespoon **tamarind paste**

Process the spice paste ingredients up to and including the chillies in a blender or food processor until roughly chopped, or pound using a mortar and pestle. Add the lemon grass and onions, and process or pound to a dry paste. Add the tamarind paste and blend together.

Heat the oil in a large saucepan over a medium-high heat. Working in batches, fry the beef for a few minutes until browned on all sides. Remove each batch with a slotted spoon and set aside on a plate. Add the spice paste to the hot pan, and fry for 2–3 minutes, stirring constantly. Return the reserved beef to the pan with all the remaining ingredients, reduce the heat slightly and bring slowly to the boil, stirring constantly.

Reduce the heat again to as low as possible, and simmer very gently for 4–4½ hours, stirring occasionally, until the meat is tender and the sauce has reduced and thickened – the flavour improves with slow cooking.

Increase the heat when the sauce is very thick to make a true 'dry' rendang, if liked. Stirring constantly, fry the beef in the thick sauce until it is a rich brown colour and almost dry, and nearly all of the sauce has been absorbed. Serve hot.

For egg rendang, omit the beef from the recipe and fry 1 roughly chopped onion and 2 potatoes, cut into large dice, for 5 minutes instead. Add the spice paste and remaining ingredients. Simmer for 1 hour, then remove the potatoes and set aside. Continue cooking until the sauce has reduced and thickened. Return the potatoes to the pan with 6 hard-boiled eggs, peeled and halved, and cook for 5 minutes to heat through.

aubergine, basil & ricotta pizza

Serves **4**
Preparation time **10 minutes**
Cooking time **50 minutes**

150 ml (¼ pint) **passata**
  (sieved tomatoes)
5 large **basil leaves**, torn, plus
  extra leaves, to garnish
1 **garlic clove**, crushed
2–3 small–medium
  aubergines, cut lengthways
  into 5 mm (¼ inch) thick
  slices
4 fresh **pizza bases**
125 g (4 oz) **ricotta cheese**,
  broken into small chunks
75 g (3 oz) **mozzarella
  cheese** (drained weight),
  roughly chopped
olive oil for glazing
salt

Combine the passata, torn basil leaves and garlic in a bowl. Season lightly with salt, cover and leave to infuse while you cook the aubergines.

Heat a ridged griddle pan over a high heat until smoking hot. Add the aubergine, in batches, and cook for 2 minutes on each side until charred on the outside and soft all the way through.

Put a baking sheet in a preheated oven, 240°C (475°F), Gas Mark 9, to heat through. Place 1 pizza base on the base only of a well-floured 23 cm (9 inch) loose-bottomed tart tin.

Spoon 2 tablespoons of the passata mixture over the base, top with a quarter of the aubergines, then scatter with a quarter each of the cheeses. Brush the border with oil, to glaze. Remove the heated baking sheet from the oven, slide the tin on to it, then quickly return to the oven. Bake for 7–8 minutes until crisp and risen. Serve immediately, garnished with basil leaves. As the first pizza cooks, prepare the next for the oven.

For courgette & smoked mozzarella pizza, replace the aubergines with 4 courgettes, cut lengthways into 5 mm (¼ inch) thick slices, and griddle as above. Omit the ricotta and mozzarella cheeses, and replace with 150 g (5 oz) sliced smoked mozzarella or caciocavallo cheese.

chicken teriyaki

Serves **4**
Preparation time **10 minutes**
Cooking time **10 minutes**

625 g (1 ¼ lb) **boneless,
  skinless chicken
  breasts**, cubed
about 8 **spring onions**, cut
  into 5 cm (2 inch) lengths,
  plus 1 extra, finely chopped,
  to garnish
2 **red peppers**, cored,
  deseeded and cut
  into chunks
2 tablespoons **vegetable oil**

Teriyaki sauce
3 tablespoons **Japanese soy
  sauce** or **Chinese dark soy
  sauce**
3 tablespoons **clear honey**
3 tablespoons **sake** or **dry
  sherry**
1 **garlic clove**, crushed
3 slices of peeled **fresh root
  ginger**

Put all the sauce ingredients in a small saucepan,
and simmer for 5 minutes until thickened.

Meanwhile, divide the chicken cubes, spring onion
lengths and red peppers evenly among 8 metal
skewers, threading the ingredients alternately. Brush
with oil.

Heat a ridged griddle pan until hot. Arrange the chicken
skewers in the pan and cook for 4 minutes on each side
or until cooked through. Alternatively, cook under
a preheated very hot grill.

Brush the skewers with the teriyaki sauce, drizzle with
more sauce and serve with boiled rice, sprinkled with
the extra chopped spring onion.

For marinated miso chicken, mix together 3
tablespoons miso paste, 2 tablespoons clear honey
and 4 tablespoons sake or dry sherry. Add the diced
chicken and crushed garlic, omitting the ginger, and
marinate in the refrigerator for at least 30 minutes.
Thread alternately on to skewers with the spring
onions and peppers. Cook as above, brushing with
the marinade from time to time.

melanzane parmigiana

Serves **6**
Preparation time **40 minutes**
Cooking time **50 minutes,
  plus standing**

6 **aubergines**
2 tablespoons **olive oil**
250 g (8 oz) grated **Cheddar
  cheese**
50 g (2 oz) grated
  Parmesan cheese
salt

Tomato sauce
2 tablespoons **olive oil**
1 large **onion,** chopped
2 **garlic cloves,** finely chopped
14 oz can **chopped tomatoes**
salt and **pepper**

Make the tomato sauce, by first heating the olive oil in a frying pan. Fry the onion for 5 minutes, then add the garlic, add the tomatoes and cook, gently, for 10 minutes. Season well and keep warm.

Trim the ends off the aubergines and cut them lengthways into thick slices. Sprinkle generously with salt and set side for about 10 minutes. Wash well, drain and pat dry on kitchen paper.

Brush the aubergine slices with oil, and place them on 2 large baking sheets. Roast the aubergines in a preheated oven, 200°C (400°F), Gas Mark 6, for 10 minutes on each side until golden and tender. Do not turn off the oven.

Spoon a little of the tomato sauce into an ovenproof dish, and top with a layer of roasted aubergine and some of the Cheddar. Continue with the layers, finishing with the Cheddar. Sprinkle over the Parmesan, and bake for 30 minutes until bubbling and golden. Remove from the oven, and leave to stand for 5–10 minutes. Serve with a crisp green salad and crusty bread to mop up the juices.

For aubergines with mozzarella & mint, bake the aubergines and make the tomato sauce as above. Layer alternately in an ovenproof dish with 2 x 150 g (5 oz) drained and sliced mozzarella cheeses and 2 tablespoons chopped mint. Sprinkle the top layer with 50 g (2 oz) grated Parmesan cheese and bake as above.

tuna & sweetcorn pilaf

Serves **4**
Preparation time **10 minutes**
Cooking time **15–20 minutes**

2 tablespoons **olive oil**
1 **onion**, chopped
1 **red pepper**, cored,
    deseeded and diced
1 **garlic clove**, crushed
250 g (8 oz) **easy-cook
    long-grain rice**
750 ml (1¼ pints) **chicken
    stock**
325 g (11 oz) can **sweetcorn**,
    drained
200 g (7 oz) can **tuna in
    spring water**, drained
salt and **pepper**
6 chopped **spring onions**, to
    garnish

Put the oil in a saucepan over a low heat. Add the onion and red pepper and cook gently for about 5 minutes until softened. Add the garlic and cook for another 30 seconds. Stir in the rice, then pour over the stock and season with salt and pepper.

Bring to the boil, then reduce the heat and simmer, stirring occasionally, for 10–15 minutes until all the stock has been absorbed and the rice is tender.

Stir in the sweetcorn and tuna, and cook briefly over a low heat to heat through. Serve immediately garnished with the spring onions.

For picnic pilaf cake, put the cooked rice mixture in a 23 cm (9 inch) square nonstick cake tin. In a bowl, whisk together 4 eggs and 4 tablespoons finely chopped flat leaf parsley. Season well with salt and pepper and pour over the rice mixture. Bake in a preheated oven, 180°C (350°F), Gas Mark 4, for 25–30 minutes until set. Leave to cool, then remove from the tin and serve cut into thick wedges.

quick pasta carbonara

Serves **4**
Preparation time **10 minutes**
Cooking time **10 minutes**

400 g (13 oz) **dried spaghetti**
or other long, thin pasta
2 tablespoons **olive oil**
200 g (7 oz) **pancetta**, cut
into cubes
3 **eggs**
4 tablespoons freshly grated
Parmesan cheese
3 tablespoons chopped **flat
leaf parsley**
3 tablespoons **single cream**
salt and **pepper**

Cook the pasta in a large saucepan of boiling salted water according to the packet instructions until al dente.

Meanwhile, heat the oil in a large nonstick frying pan over a medium heat. Add the pancetta and cook, stirring frequently, for 4–5 minutes until crisp.

Whisk together the eggs, Parmesan, parsley and cream in a bowl. Season with salt and pepper and set aside.

Drain the pasta and add to the pancetta in the frying pan. Stir over a low heat until combined, then pour in the egg mixture. Stir and remove the pan from the heat. Continue stirring for a few seconds until the eggs are lightly cooked and creamy. Serve immediately.

For blue cheese & bacon carbonara, cook the spaghetti as above. Fry 200 g (7 oz) diced smoked streaky bacon in 2 tablespoons olive oil until golden. Add the drained pasta, 125 g (4 oz) crumbled Stilton or Danish blue cheese, 3 tablespoons chopped flat leaf parsley and 3 tablespoons single cream. Season with a little salt and pepper. Cook and serve as above.

leeks baked with blue cheese

Serves **4**
Preparation time **5 minutes**
Cooking time **30–35 minutes**

750 g (1½ lb) **leeks**, trimmed,
cleaned and cut into 3 and
halved lengthways
2 tablespoons **hazelnut oil**
4 tablespoons **vegetable
stock**
15 g (½ oz) **butter**
125 g (4 oz) **Dolcelatte
cheese**, crumbled
2 tablespoons toasted
blanched hazelnuts,
chopped
salt and **pepper**

Toss the leeks with the oil in a bowl, then put in
a shallow ovenproof dish with the stock. Bake in a
preheated oven, 200°C (400°F), Gas Mark 6, for
15 minutes.

Dot the leeks with the butter, cheese and nuts, then
return to the oven and cook for another 15–20 minutes
until the leeks are tender, the cheese has melted and
the hazelnuts are golden. Sprinkle with salt and pepper
and serve immediately.

For creamy leeks with Cheddar, prepare the leeks
as above. Put in an ovenproof dish with 1 chopped
garlic clove and pour over 300 ml (½ pint) double
cream. Season with salt and pepper. Sprinkle with
2 tablespoons grated Cheddar cheese and bake for
25–30 minutes, or until golden.

salmon with horseradish crust

Serves **4**
Preparation time **10 minutes**
Cooking time **12–15 minutes**

4 **salmon fillets,** about 200 g
   (7 oz) each, skin on and
   pin-boned
4 tablespoons **mild**
   horseradish sauce
125 g (4 oz) **fresh**
   breadcrumbs
20 **fresh asparagus spears,**
   trimmed
1 tablespoon **olive oil**
4–5 tablespoons **crème**
   fraîche
4 tablespoons **lemon juice**
1 tablespoon chopped **flat**
   leaf parsley
salt and **pepper**

Place the salmon fillets in an ovenproof dish, skin side down. Spread the top of each fillet with 1 tablespoon of the horseradish sauce, then sprinkle with the breadcrumbs. Roast in a preheated oven, 180°C (350°F), Gas Mark 4, for 12–15 minutes until the fish is just cooked and the breadcrumbs are golden brown.

Meanwhile, blanch the asparagus in salted boiling water for 2 minutes, then drain. Place in a very hot ridged griddle pan with the oil and grill for a couple of minutes on each side until slightly charred and just tender. Season with salt and pepper.

Mix together the crème fraîche, lemon juice and parsley in a small bowl and season with salt and pepper.

Serve the salmon with the char-grilled asparagus and lemon crème fraîche.

For roasted salmon with horseradish sauce, season the salmon with salt and pepper and roast in the oven as above. Add 1 finely chopped shallot to a little olive oil in a pan and cook until softened. Remove from the heat and add 2 tablespoons horseradish sauce and 6 tablespoons crème fraîche. Season with salt and pepper. Serve with the roasted salmon.

ginger beef with peppers

Serves **3–4**

Preparation time **10 minutes**, plus marinating

Cooking time **about 5 minutes**

500 g (1lb) lean **rump** or **fillet steak**, thinly sliced

2 teaspoons **light soy sauce**

2 tablespoons **sesame oil**

2.5 cm (1 inch) piece of **fresh root ginger**, peeled and sliced

2 teaspoons **rice vinegar**

1 tablespoon **water**

1 teaspoon **salt**

1 teaspoon **cornflour**

1 **garlic clove**, crushed

pinch of **five-spice powder**

1 **red pepper**, cored, deseeded and cut into chunks

1 **green pepper**, cored, deseeded and cut into chunks

slivers of **fresh red chilli**, to garnish (optional)

Put the slices of steak in a bowl and add the soy sauce, 1 teaspoon of the sesame oil, ginger, vinegar, measurement water, salt and cornflour. Stir well to mix and thoroughly coat the steak slices. Cover and leave to marinate in the refrigerator for at least 20 minutes.

Heat the remaining sesame oil in a wok or frying pan over a high heat. Add the garlic and five-spice powder. Stir-fry for 30 seconds until the garlic is just opaque, then add the marinated steak; reserve any remaining marinade. Stir-fry the beef quickly for a couple of minutes until it is browned on the outside yet pink and tender on the inside, working in batches if necessary to avoid 'stewing' the meat. Remove and set aside.

Add the red and green peppers to the wok or frying pan and stir-fry briskly for 2–3 minutes, tossing them in the oil. Return the steak and the reserved marinade to the pan. Stir-fry for 1 minute until the meat is heated through. Transfer to a serving dish and garnish with thin slivers of chilli, if liked. Serve immediately with straight-to-wok noodles or boiled rice.

For gingered tofu with peppers, thickly slice 500 g (1 lb) well-drained chilled tofu and arrange on a foil-lined grill rack. Mix 1 tablespoon sesame oil, 3 tablespoons light soy sauce and a 2.5 cm (1 inch) piece of finely chopped root ginger in a bowl and spoon over the top of the tofu. Leave to marinate for 20 minutes, then grill for 4–5 minutes under a preheated hot grill, turning once. Meanwhile, heat 1 tablespoon sesame oil in a wok, add the garlic, five-spice powder and red and green peppers as above and stir-fry for 2–3 minutes. Add the tofu, toss through and serve hot sprinkled with fresh chilli, if liked.

carrot, pea & broad bean risotto

Serves **4**
Preparation time **15 minutes**
Cooking time **about 30 minutes**

1.5 litres (2½ pints) **vegetable stock**
4 tablespoons **butter**
2 tablespoons **olive oil**
1 large **onion**, finely chopped
2 **carrots**, finely chopped
2 **garlic cloves**, finely chopped
350 g (11½ oz) **risotto rice**
200 ml (7 fl oz) **white wine**
200 g (7 oz) **frozen peas**, thawed
100 g (3½ oz) **frozen broad beans**, thawed and peeled
50 g (2 oz) **Parmesan cheese**, finely grated
handful of **flat leaf parsley**, roughly chopped
salt and **pepper**

Pour the stock into a saucepan and heat until just simmering. Keep hot.

Melt the butter with the oil in a saucepan over a low heat. Add the onion and carrots and cook gently for about 5 minutes until the onion is soft and translucent. Add the garlic and cook for another 1 minute until the garlic is opaque. Stir in the rice and continue stirring for a couple of minutes until the grains are coated with the butter mixture. Pour in the wine and cook rapidly, stirring, until the alcohol has evaporated.

Add the hot stock, a ladleful at a time, and cook over a low heat, stirring constantly, until each addition has been absorbed before adding the next. Continue until all the stock has been absorbed and the rice is creamy and cooked, but still retains a little bite – this will take around 15 minutes. (Be careful not to overcook.)

Add the peas and broad beans and heat through for 3–5 minutes. Remove from the heat and stir in the Parmesan and chopped parsley. Season with salt and pepper and serve immediately.

For Italian-style risotto balls, leave the risotto to cool, then chill overnight in the refrigerator. Form the chilled mixture into walnut-sized balls. Whisk together 2 eggs in a shallow bowl. Roll the rice balls through the egg, then in 100 g (3½ oz) dried breadcrumbs to coat. Fill a deep heavy-based saucepan one-third full with vegetable oil and heat to 180°–190°C (350°–375°F), or until a cube of bread browns in 30 seconds. Add the rice balls, in batches, and cook for 2–3 minutes until golden. Remove with a slotted spoon, drain on kitchen paper and serve.

prawn laksa

Serves **1**
Preparation time **20 minutes**
Cooking time **15 minutes**

100 g (3½ oz) **rice noodles**
1 teaspoon **olive oil**
½ **red pepper**, cored,
   deseeded and sliced
100 g (3½ oz) **mushrooms**,
   sliced
1 teaspoon **laksa paste** or
   Thai red or **green curry**
   paste
150 ml (¼ pint) **fish stock**
150 ml (¼ pint) **coconut milk**
100 g (3½ oz) **raw tiger**
   prawns, peeled and
   deveined
2 **spring onions**, sliced
1 tablespoon chopped **fresh**
   coriander

Put the noodles in a bowl, cover with boiling water and leave to soften for about 5 minutes or according to the packet instructions (the time needed for soaking will depend on the thickness of the noodles you use). Drain in a colander, rinse under cold water and set aside.

Heat the oil in a saucepan over a medium heat. Add the red pepper and mushrooms, and cook for 3–4 minutes until softened. Add the laksa or curry paste and cook, stirring, for 1 minute until fragrant.

Pour in the stock and coconut milk, and bring to the boil. Reduce the heat and simmer for 5 minutes.

Add the prawns, spring onions, drained noodles and coriander, stir to mix and cook for 3–4 minutes until the prawns have turned pink and are just cooked through. Serve immediately.

For tuna & pea laksa, prepare the noodles as above. Fry the mushrooms in the oil, omitting the pepper, then add the curry paste, followed by the stock, coconut milk and 100 g (3½ oz) frozen peas. Simmer for 5 minutes, then mix in a 200 g (7 oz) can drained tuna instead of the prawns, adding the spring onions, drained noodles and coriander. Simmer for 3–4 minutes until heated through.

pork & rosemary pasta sauce

Serves **4**
Preparation time **20 minutes**
Cooking time **45 minutes**

3 tablespoons **olive oil**, plus
   extra, for drizzling
½ **onion**, finely chopped
1 **carrot**, finely diced
2 **celery sticks**, finely diced
2 **garlic cloves**, finely chopped
350 g (12 oz) **pork fillet**, cut
   into 1 cm (½ inch) cubes
2 teaspoons finely chopped
   rosemary, plus few leaves to
   garnish (optional)
finely grated rind of ½ **lemon**
400 g (13 oz) can **chopped
   tomatoes**
200 ml (7 fl oz) **chicken stock**
salt and **pepper**
50 g (2 oz) **Parmesan
   cheese**, freshly grated,
   to serve

Heat the oil in a saucepan over a low heat and gently fry the onion for 5 minutes until soft and golden. Add the carrot, celery and garlic and fry gently for another 5 minutes.

Stir in the pork, rosemary and lemon rind, and fry for a few minutes until the pork is lightly browned all over. Season with salt and pepper.

Add the tomatoes and stock. Bring to the boil, then gently simmer over a low heat for 30 minutes. Serve hot with rigatoni or penne pasta, drizzled with a little extra olive oil and garnished with the rosemary, if liked. Serve the grated Parmesan in a bowl at the table for sprinkling over the top.

For pork & basil gnocchi, follow the recipe as above, frying the pork with the lemon rind and 2 tablespoons roughly torn basil leaves instead of the rosemary. Add the tomatoes and stock and continue cooking the meat sauce as above. Toss with 500 g (1 lb) ready-made vacuum-packed gnocchi that has been cooked in a saucepan of boiling water according to the packet instructions and drained well.

76

lemon chicken with yogurt sauce

Serves **4**

Preparation time **10 minutes**,
    plus marinating

Cooking time **35–45 minutes**

4 **chicken quarters**

2 **lemons**, cut in half

1 tablespoon **dried oregano**

2 sprigs of **thyme**

4 tablespoons **olive oil**

4 **garlic cloves**, roughly
    chopped

Yogurt sauce

250 ml (8 fl oz) **thick
    Greek yogurt**

1–2 **garlic cloves**

½ teaspoon **salt**

1 tablespoon chopped **dill**

Rub the chicken quarters all over, quite hard, with the cut lemons. Place the chicken quarters in a bowl or shallow dish. Add the oregano, thyme, olive oil, garlic and rubbed lemon halves and mix everything together well. Cover with clingfilm and leave to marinate in the refrigerator for at least 2 hours.

Meanwhile, make the yogurt sauce. Pour the yogurt into a bowl and beat until smooth. Mash together the garlic and salt in a bowl, then stir into the yogurt with the dill. Set aside.

Transfer the marinated chicken to a roasting tin and roast in a preheated oven, 200°C (400°F), Gas Mark 6, for 35–45 minutes, spooning over a bit of the marinade now and then if the chicken looks too dry or burnt. To test whether the chicken is cooked through, pierce at the thickest point with a skewer – if the juices run clear, it is ready.

Serve with the yogurt sauce and a big plate of piping-hot chips and salad leaves.

For chicken salad with yogurt sauce, cook the chicken as above, then leave to cool. Take the meat off the bones and cut into chunks. Mix into the yogurt sauce. Divide a 125 g (4 oz) bag of mixed salad leaves among 4 plates, then spoon the chicken salad on top. Alternatively, spoon into toasted and split pitta breads, if liked.

mango & prawn curry

Serves **4**
Preparation time **10 minutes**
Cooking time **25 minutes**

3 **garlic cloves**, crushed
2 teaspoons finely grated
  fresh root ginger
2 tablespoons **ground**
  coriander
2 teaspoons **ground cumin**
1 teaspoon **chilli powder**
1 teaspoon **paprika**
½ teaspoon **ground turmeric**
1 tablespoon **grated jaggery**
  or **palm sugar** or **soft light**
  brown sugar
400 ml (14 fl oz) **water**
1 **green mango**, stoned and
  thinly sliced
400 ml (14 fl oz) **half-fat**
  coconut milk
1 tablespoon **tamarind paste**
600 g (1¼ lb) **raw tiger**
  prawns, peeled and
  deveined
1 small bunch of **fresh**
  coriander
salt

Put the garlic, ginger, ground coriander, cumin, chilli powder, paprika, turmeric and jaggery or sugar in a large wok. Pour in the measurement water and stir to mix well. Place the wok over a high heat and bring the mixture to the boil. Reduce the heat and cook, covered, for 8–10 minutes.

Add the mango, coconut milk and tamarind paste and stir to combine. Bring the mixture back to the boil, then add the prawns.

Stir reduce the heat and simmer gently for 6–8 minutes. Tear some of the coriander leaves into the curry (reserve the rest to use as a garnish) and cook for another 2 minutes until the prawns have turned pink and are just cooked through. Season with a little salt and serve immediately with steamed basmati rice, garnished with the reserved sprigs of coriander.

For chicken & sweet potato curry, simmer the spices in the measurement water as above. Omit the mango and prawns and add 1 small peeled and diced sweet potato and 500 g (1 lb) diced boneless, skinless chicken breasts with the coconut milk and 1 tablespoon tamarind paste. Bring to the boil, reduce the heat and simmer gently for 20 minutes until the chicken is cooked through. Add the coriander and serve as above.

lentil moussaka

Serves **4**
Preparation time **10 minutes**
Cooking time **45 minutes**,
  plus standing

125 g (4 oz) **brown** or **green
  lentils**, picked over, rinsed
  and drained
400 g (13 oz) can **chopped
  tomatoes**
2 **garlic cloves**, crushed
½ teaspoon **dried oregano**
pinch of **ground nutmeg**
150 ml (¼ pint) **vegetable
  stock**
2–3 tablespoons
  vegetable oil
250 g (8 oz) **aubergine**, sliced
1 **onion**, finely chopped

Cheese topping
1 **egg**
150 g (5 oz) **soft cheese**
pinch of **ground nutmeg**
salt and **pepper**

Put the lentils in a saucepan with the tomatoes, garlic, oregano and nutmeg. Pour in the stock. Bring to the boil, then reduce the heat and simmer for 20 minutes until the lentils are tender but not mushy, topping up with extra stock as needed.

Meanwhile heat the oil in a frying pan and lightly fry the aubergine and onion, until the onion is soft and the aubergine is golden on both sides.

Layer the aubergine mixture and lentil mixture alternately in an ovenproof dish.

Make the topping. In a bowl, beat together the egg, cheese and nutmeg with a good dash of salt and pepper. Pour over the moussaka and cook in a preheated oven, 200°C (400°F), Gas Mark 6, for 20–25 minutes.

Remove from the oven and leave to stand for 5 minutes before serving with salad leaves.

For moussaka jacket potatoes, cook 4 scrubbed baking potatoes in a preheated oven, 200°C (400°F), Gas Mark 6, for about 1 hour until tender, or microwave if preferred. Meanwhile, make the lentil mixture as above. Fry the aubergine and onion separately, then stir into the lentils when cooked. Spoon over the slit potatoes, then top each one with a spoonful of soft cheese and a sprinkling of grated Cheddar cheese.

chicken thighs with fresh pesto

Serves **4**
Preparation time **5 minutes**
Cooking time **25 minutes**

1 tablespoon **olive oil**
8 **boneless, skinless chicken thighs**

Pesto
90 ml (3 fl oz) **olive oil**
50 g (2 oz) **pine nuts**, toasted
50 g (2 oz) **Parmesan cheese**, freshly grated
50 g (2 oz) **basil leaves**, plus extra to garnish
15 g (½ oz) **flat leaf parsley**, roughly chopped
2 **garlic cloves**, chopped
salt and **pepper**

Heat the oil in a nonstick frying pan over a medium heat, add the chicken thighs and pan-fry gently, turning frequently, for 20 minutes or until cooked through.

Put all the the pesto, put all the ingredients in a blender or food processor and blend until smooth.

Remove the chicken from the pan and set aside to keep warm. Reduce the heat to as low as possible, add the pesto and heat through very gently for 2–3 minutes.

Pour the warmed pesto over the chicken thighs, garnish with extra basil and serve with roasted Mediterranean vegetables (see below), steamed vegetables or a spinach salad.

For roasted Mediterranean vegetables, add 500 g (1 lb) scrubbed baby new potatoes to a roasting tin, halving any large ones. Add ½ red pepper and ½ yellow pepper, both cored, deseeded and cut into chunks, 1 red onion, cut into chunks, 1 sliced large courgette and 2–3 roughly chopped garlic cloves. Drizzle with 3 tablespoons olive oil and roast in a preheated oven, 200°C (400°F), Gas Mark 6, for 30 minutes, turning once, until the potatoes are golden.

farfalle with tuna sauce

Serves **4**

Preparation time **10 minutes**, plus infusing

Cooking time **about 12 minutes**

125 g (4 oz) **canned tuna in olive oil**, drained

2 tablespoons **extra virgin olive oil**, plus extra, for drizzling (optional)

4 ripe **tomatoes**, roughly chopped

50 g (2 oz) **pitted black olives**, roughly chopped

grated rind of 1 **lemon**

2 **garlic cloves**, crushed

2 tablespoons roughly chopped **flat leaf parsley**

350 g (11½ oz) **dried farfalle pasta**

salt

Put the drained tuna in a large serving bowl. Break it up with a fork, then stir in the remaining ingredients except for the pasta. Season with salt, cover and leave to stand for at least 30 minutes (including the pasta's cooking time), to allow the flavours to infuse.

Cook the pasta in a large saucepan of salted boiling water according to the packet instructions until al dente, then drain. Toss with the tuna mixture. Serve immediately with a drizzle of extra virgin olive oil, if liked.

For farfalle with salami & basil sauce, mix 2 tablespoons olive oil with 2 teaspoons ready-made pesto. Add 75 g (3 oz) diced salami and 100 g (3½ oz) sliced mushrooms and stir through. Next, add 4 chopped tomatoes, the grated rind of 1 lemon, 2 crushed garlic cloves and 2 tablespoons roughly chopped fresh basil or flat leaf parsley. Toss with the cooked and drained pasta as above.

grilled pork steaks with sage

Serves **4**

Preparation time **5 minutes**,
   plus marinating

Cooking time **10 minutes**

4 **pork loin steaks**, about
   200 g (7 oz) each
2 **garlic cloves**, finely chopped
1 ½ tablespoons finely
   chopped **sage**
1 teaspoon **olive oil**
salt and **pepper**

Cut a horizontal pocket through the centre of each pork steak.

Combine the garlic, sage and oil in a small bowl, then rub this mixture all over the outside and inside of the pork steaks. Place in a shallow dish, cover with clingfilm and leave to marinate in the refrigerator for at least 30 minutes or overnight.

Season the outside and inside of the pork steaks with salt and pepper, then place on a baking sheet lined with foil. Cook under a preheated very hot grill, about 10 cm (4 inches) from the heat, for 5 minutes. Turn the pork steaks over and cook for another 5 minutes or until cooked through and golden. Serve with sweet potato mash, or ordinary mash if you prefer.

For pork steaks with sage & polenta, trim any excess fat from 8 thin-cut pork loin steaks, about 100 g (3½ oz) each. Mix 250 g (8 oz) instant polenta with 50 g (2 oz) freshly grated Parmesan cheese and 1 ½ tablespoons chopped sage. Beat 2 eggs in a shallow dish, dip the pork steaks into the beaten egg, then coat in the polenta mixture. Pan-fry the steaks in 2–3 tablespoons olive oil for 15 minutes, turning until golden and cooked through. Serve with salad.

classic favourites

classic bolognese

Serves **4**
Preparation time **10 minutes**
Cooking time **4–6 hours**

25 g (1 oz) **unsalted butter**
1 tablespoon **olive oil**
1 small **onion**, finely chopped
2 **celery sticks**, finely chopped
1 **carrot**, finely chopped
1 **bay leaf**
200 g (7 oz) **lean minced beef**
200 g (7 oz) **lean minced pork**
150 ml (¼ pint) **dry white wine**
150 ml (¼ pint) **milk**
large pinch of freshly grated **nutmeg**
2 x 400 g (13 oz) cans **chopped tomatoes**
400–600 ml (14 fl oz–1 pint) **chicken stock**
400 g (13 oz) dried or fresh **tagliatelle** or **fettuccine**
salt and **pepper**
freshly grated **Parmesan cheese**, to serve

Melt the butter with the oil in a large heavy-based saucepan over a low heat. Add the onion, celery, carrot and bay leaf. Cook, stirring occasionally, for 10 minutes until softened but not coloured. Add the meat, season with salt and pepper and cook over a medium heat, stirring and breaking up the meat with a wooden spoon, until no longer pink.

Pour in the wine and bring to the boil. Gently simmer for 15 minutes until evaporated. Stir in the milk and nutmeg, and simmer for a further 15 minutes until the milk has evaporated. Stir in the tomatoes and simmer very gently, uncovered, over a very low heat for 3–5 hours. The sauce is very thick, so when it begins to stick, add 100 ml (3½ fl oz) of the stock at a time, as needed.

Cook the pasta in a large saucepan of salted boiling water until al dente: according to the packet instructions for dried pasta or for 2 minutes if you are using fresh pasta. Drain thoroughly, reserving a ladleful of the cooking water.

Return the pasta to the pan and place over a low heat. Add the sauce and stir for 30 seconds, then pour in the reserved pasta cooking water and stir until the pasta is well coated and looks silky. Serve immediately with a scattering of grated Parmesan.

For rich pork & chicken liver bolognese, dice
100 g (3½ oz) chicken liver and 100 g (3½ oz) pancetta and cook with the onion and celery mixture as above. Omit the beef and use 400 g (14 oz) minced pork and proceed as in the recipe above.

chicken & mushroom pie

Serves **4**

Preparation time **20 minutes**

Cooking time **about 35
minutes**

2 tablespoons **vegetable oil**

1 **onion**, chopped

1 **garlic clove**, crushed

125 g (4 oz) **mushrooms**,
sliced

1 tablespoon **plain flour**

300 ml (½ pint) **chicken stock**

500 g (1 lb) **cooked chicken**,
cut into cubes

1 tablespoon chopped **flat
leaf parsley**

375 g (12 oz) **ready-made
puff pastry** (preferably made
with butter), thawed if frozen

beaten egg, to glaze

salt and **pepper**

Heat the oil in a frying pan over a medium heat.
Add the onion and fry for about 5 minutes, stirring
occasionally, until soft and translucent. Add the garlic
and mushrooms and cook for another 2 minutes.

Remove the pan from the heat and stir in the flour.
Slowly add the stock, a little at a time, and stir until well
mixed. Return the pan to the heat and bring to the boil,
stirring until thick and smooth.

Stir in the cooked chicken and parsley. Season with
salt and pepper. Mix well, then put in a 1.2 litre (2 pint)
pie dish or similar-sized ovenproof dish.

Roll out the pastry on a lightly floured surface to a
shape just larger than the dish and put it over the
pie. Brush the edge of the pie dish with beaten egg,
add the pastry lid, press on to the dish edge then
trim any excess pastry. Push down the edges to seal,
crimping the edges with a finger and a small knife.
Using a sharp knife, decorate the top of the pastry with
crisscross lines, brush with the beaten egg and bake in
a preheated oven, 200°C (400°F), Gas Mark 6, for 30
minutes until the pastry is puffed and golden brown.

For chicken & mushroom potato pie, peel and cut
500 g (1 lb) floury potatoes and 250 g (8 oz) swede
into chunks. Cook in a saucepan of boiling water for
15 minutes until tender. Drain, tip back into the pan
and mash with 25 g (1 oz) butter and 3 tablespoons
milk. Season with salt and pepper. Spoon over the hot
chicken and mushroom filling in the pie dish, dot with
25 g (1 oz) extra butter and cook under a preheated
very hot grill for a few minutes until golden. Serve hot.

fish & chips

Serves **4**
Preparation time **25 minutes**
Cooking time **30 minutes**

125 g (4 oz) **self-raising flour**,
  plus extra for dusting
½ teaspoon **baking powder**
¼ teaspoon **ground turmeric**
200 ml (7 fl oz) **cold water**
1.5 kg (3 lb) large **floury**
  potatoes such as Maris
  Piper or King Edward
750 g (1½ lb) piece of **cod** or
  haddock fillet, skinned and
  pin-boned
sunflower oil, for deep-frying
salt and **pepper**

Mix together the flour, baking powder, turmeric and a pinch of salt in a bowl and make a well in the centre. Pour half the measurement water into it. Gradually whisk the flour into the water to make a smooth batter, then whisk in the remaining water. Set aside.

Cut the potatoes into 1.5 cm (¾ inch) slices, then cut across to make chunky chips. Put them in a bowl of cold water. Pat the fish dry on kitchen paper and cut into 4 portions. Season lightly with salt and pepper and dust with extra flour. Thoroughly drain the chips and pat them dry on kitchen paper. Pour the oil into a deep-fat fryer or deep, heavy-based saucepan to a depth of at least 7 cm (3 inches) and heat to 180°–190°C (350°–375°F), or until a teaspoonful of batter turns golden in 30 seconds. Fry half the chips for 10 minutes or until golden. Drain and keep warm while you cook the remainder. Keep all the chips warm while you fry the fish.

Dip 2 pieces of fish in the batter, then carefully lower them into the hot oil. Fry gently for 4–5 minutes until crisp and golden. Drain and keep warm while you fry the rest. Serve with the chips.

For tomato chutney, to serve as an accompaniment, roughly chop 1.25 kg (2½ lb) tomatoes and finely chop 1 onion. Tip into a saucepan, including any juices from the tomatoes, with 150 g (5 oz) caster sugar and 150 ml (¼ pint) malt vinegar. Bring to the boil, then reduce the heat and simmer gently for 1 hour or until sticky, stirring frequently. Pot the chutney into hot sterilized jars, cover with vinegar-proof lids and seal tightly. Allow to cool, then store in a cool, dark place. Keep refrigerated once opened.

spinach & potato omelette

Serves **4–6**

Preparation time **10 minutes**, plus cooling

Cooking time **about 45 minutes**

250 g (8 oz) **waxy potatoes** such as Charlotte, peeled and cut into 1.5 cm (¾ inch) dice

200 g (7 oz) **baby spinach leaves**

2 tablespoons **olive oil**

1 small **onion**, finely chopped

6 large **eggs**

salt and **pepper**

Cook the potatoes in a saucepan of lightly salted boiling water until just tender; be careful not to overcook. Drain, then leave to cool.

Rinse the spinach and drain off the excess water in a colander. Put in a dry frying pan over a medium heat with just the water clinging to the leaves from rinsing, cover and cook for 2–3 minutes, shaking the pan from time to time, until just wilted. Squeeze out any remaining water, then roughly chop. Set aside.

Heat the oil in a 20 cm (8 inch) nonstick frying pan with a flameproof handle (or cover the handle with foil) over a low heat. Add the onion and cook, stirring occasionally, for 8–10 minutes until softened. Add the cooled potatoes and cook, stirring, for 2–3 minutes. Add the reserved spinach and stir. Beat the eggs lightly in a bowl and season with salt and pepper. Pour into the pan over the vegetables and cook over a low heat, shaking frequently, for 10–12 minutes until set on the bottom.

Put the pan under a preheated medium grill and cook for 2–3 minutes or until the top is set and lightly browned. Remove from the heat and leave to rest for 3–4 minutes before turning out on to a chopping board. Cut into wedges and serve with plain or chilli ketchup.

For bacon & pea omelette, omit the spinach and fry 1 chopped onion with 4 diced smoked streaky bacon rashers in the oil. Add the cooked diced potatoes as above, fry for 2–3 minutes, then add 75 g (3 oz) frozen green peas. Cook for 2 minutes. Beat together the eggs and salt and pepper with 1 tablespoon chopped mint, if liked. Add to the pan and cook as above.

shepherd's pie

Serves **4–6**
Preparation time **20 minutes**
Cooking time **about 1½ hours**

1 tablespoon **olive oil**
1 **onion**, finely chopped
1 **carrot**, diced
1 **celery stick**, diced
1 tablespoon chopped **thyme**
500 g (1 lb) **minced lamb**
400 g (13 oz) can **chopped tomatoes**
4 tablespoons **tomato purée**
750 g (1½ lb) **floury potatoes** such as Maris Piper or King Edward, peeled and cubed
50 g (2 oz) **butter**
3 tablespoons **milk**
75 g (3 oz) **Cheddar cheese**, grated
salt and **pepper**

Heat the oil in a saucepan over a low heat. Add the onion, carrot, celery and thyme, and cook gently for 10 minutes until soft and golden. Add the minced lamb and cook over a high heat, breaking up with a wooden spoon, for 5 minutes until browned. Add the tomatoes and tomato purée. Season with salt and pepper. Bring to the boil, then reduce the heat, cover and simmer for 30 minutes. Remove the lid and cook for a further 15 minutes to thicken.

Put the potatoes in a separate large saucepan of lightly salted water and bring to the boil. Reduce the heat and simmer for 15–20 minutes, while the lamb is cooking, until really tender. Drain the potatoes well and return to the pan. Mash in the butter, milk and half the cheese, and season with salt and pepper.

Spoon the minced lamb mixture into a 2 litre (3½ pint) ovenproof dish and carefully spoon the mash over the top, spreading over the surface of the filling. Run a fork through the top of the mash to fluff up slightly and scatter over the remaining cheese. Bake in a preheated oven, 190°C (375°F), Gas Mark 5, for 20–25 minutes until bubbling and golden.

For curried lamb filo pies, prepare and cook the minced meat mixture as above, adding 1 tablespoon medium curry paste with the tomatoes and tomato purée. Spoon the filling into 6 x 300 ml (½ pint) ovenproof dishes. Omit the potato topping and instead layer 4 sheets of filo pastry together, brushing each one with a little melted butter. Cut into 6 and scrunch each over a dish to cover. Bake in a preheated oven, 190°C (375°F), Gas Mark 5, for 20 minutes until the pastry is lightly golden.

creamy pork & cider hotpot

Serves **4**
Preparation time **25 minutes**
Cooking time **1½ hours**

2 teaspoons **plain flour**
625 g (1¼ lb) **lean boneless
leg of pork**, trimmed of any
excess fat and cut into bite-
sized chunks
25 g (1 oz) **butter**
1 tablespoon **olive oil**
1 small **onion**, chopped
1 large **leek**, trimmed, cleaned
and chopped
450 ml (¾ pint) **cider**
1 tablespoon chopped **sage**
2 tablespoons **wholegrain
mustard**
2 **pears**
100 ml (3½ fl oz) **crème
fraîche**
450 g (14½ oz) **sweet
potatoes**, scrubbed and
thinly sliced
2 tablespoons **chilli oil**
salt
chopped **flat leaf parsley**,
to garnish

Season the flour with a little salt and use to coat
the pieces of meat.

Melt the butter with the oil in a shallow flameproof
casserole and gently fry the pork in batches until lightly
browned. Remove each batch with a slotted spoon and
set aside on a warm plate.

Add the onion and leek to the casserole, and fry gently
for 5 minutes until soft and translucent. Return the meat
to the pan, along with the cider, sage and mustard. Bring
just to the boil, then cover, reduce the heat to as low as
possible and simmer gently for 30 minutes.

Peel, core and thickly slice the pears. Stir the crème
fraîche into the sauce, then scatter the pear slices on
top. Arrange the sweet potato slices in overlapping
layers on top, putting the end pieces underneath and
keeping the best slices for the top layer. Brush with
the chilli oil and sprinkle with salt.

Cook in a preheated oven, 160°C (325°F), Gas Mark
3, for 45 minutes or until the potatoes are tender and
lightly browned. Scatter with the chopped parsley and
serve hot.

For creamy pork & white wine hotpot, replace the
cider with 450 ml (¾ pint) dry white wine in the third
step. Use 450 g (14½ oz) waxy potatoes instead of
the sweet potatoes, and layer on top as above. Brush
with the chilli oil and sprinkle with salt, then cook in the
oven for about 1 hour.

fast chicken curry

Serves **4**
Preparation time **5 minutes**
Cooking time **20–25 minutes**

3 tablespoons **olive oil**
1 **onion**, finely chopped
4 tablespoons **medium curry paste**
8 **boneless, skinless chicken thighs**, cut into thin strips
400 g (13 oz) can **chopped tomatoes**
250 g (8 oz) **broccoli**, broken into small florets, stalks peeled and sliced
100 ml (3½ fl oz) **coconut milk**
salt and **pepper**

Heat the oil in a deep nonstick saucepan over a medium heat. Add the onion and cook for 3 minutes until soft and translucent. Add the curry paste and cook, stirring, for 1 minute until fragrant.

Add the chicken, tomatoes, broccoli and coconut milk to the pan. Bring to the boil, then reduce the heat, cover and simmer gently over a low heat for 15–20 minutes until the chicken is cooked through.

Remove from the heat, season well with salt and pepper and serve immediately.

For seafood patties with curry sauce, follow the first stage of the recipe above, then add the tomatoes, 200 g (7 oz) young spinach leaves and the coconut milk (omitting the chicken and broccoli), and cook as directed. Meanwhile, put 375 g (12 oz) roughly chopped white fish fillets and 175 g (6 oz) frozen cooked peeled and deveined prawns, thawed and roughly chopped, in a food processor and process until well combined. Alternatively, finely chop and mix together by hand. Transfer to a bowl and add 4 finely chopped spring onions, 2 tablespoons chopped fresh coriander leaves, 50 g (2 oz) fresh white breadcrumbs, a squeeze of lemon juice and 1 beaten egg. Season with salt and pepper. Mix well, then form into 16 patties. Roll in 25 g (1 oz) fresh white breadcrumbs to coat. Heat a shallow depth of vegetable oil in a large frying pan over a medium heat. Add the patties, cooking in batches, and pan-fry for 5 minutes on each side or until crisp and golden brown an dooked through. Serve hot with the curry sauce.

quick beef stroganoff

Serves **4**
Preparation time **10 minutes**
Cooking time **15 minutes**

2 tablespoons **paprika**
1 tablespoon **plain flour**
450 g (14½ oz) **beef sirloin**, sliced
300 g (10 oz) **long-grain white rice**
25 g (1 oz) **butter**
4 tablespoons **vegetable** or **sunflower oil**
1 large **onion**, thinly sliced
250 g (8 oz) **chestnut mushrooms**, trimmed and sliced
300 ml (½ pint) **soured cream**
salt and **pepper**
1 tablespoon chopped **curly parsley**, to garnish

Mix together the paprika and flour in a large bowl. Add the beef and turn to coat.

Cook the rice in lightly salted boiling water for 13 minutes or according to the packet instructions until cooked but firm. Drain, set aside and keep warm.

Meanwhile, melt the butter with 2 tablespoons of the oil in a large frying pan over a low heat. Add the onion and cook for about 6 minutes until soft and translucent. Add the mushrooms and cook for another 5 minutes until soft. Remove with a slotted spoon and set aside.

Add the remaining oil to the pan, increase the heat to high and add the beef. Fry until browned all over, working in batches if necessary, then reduce the heat. Return the onion mixture to the pan along with the soured cream. Stir through, bring to the boil, then reduce the heat and allow to bubble gently for 1–2 minutes. Season well with salt and pepper.

Serve immediately with the cooked rice and a sprinkling of chopped parsley.

For mushroom & red pepper stroganoff, omit the beef, increase the quantity of chestnut mushrooms to 500 g (1 lb) and add 2 thinly sliced cored and deseeded red peppers. Cook the mushrooms with the onion, stirring from time to time, until they have reduced and the onion is soft and translucent. Remove the mixture from the pan with a slotted spoon. Cook the peppers in the same pan until tender, then return the onion mixture to the pan and continue as above. Sprinkle with toasted pine nuts instead of the parsley, and serve on a bed of rice.

fish pie

Serves **4**
Preparation time **15 minutes**
Cooking time **1 hour 10
   minutes**

300 g (10 oz) peeled and
   deveined **raw prawns**,
   (thawed if frozen)
2 teaspoons **cornflour**
300 g (10 oz) **white fish
   fillets** such as haddock,
   skinned and cut into
   small pieces
2 teaspoons **green
   peppercorns in brine**,
   rinsed and drained
1 small **fennel bulb**, roughly
   chopped
1 small **leek**, trimmed, cleaned
   and roughly chopped
15 g (½ oz) **dill**
15 g (½ oz) **flat leaf parsley**
100 g (3½ oz) **fresh** or **frozen
   green peas**
350 g (12 oz) **ready-made
   cheese sauce**
750 g (1½ lb) **baking
   potatoes**, thinly sliced
75 g (3 oz) **Cheddar cheese**,
   grated
salt and **pepper**

Dry the prawns, if frozen and thawed, by patting
between sheets of kitchen paper. Season the cornflour
with salt and pepper and use to coat the prawns and
white fish. Lightly crush the peppercorns using a mortar
and pestle.

Put the peppercorns in a food processor with the
fennel, leek, dill, parsley and a little salt and blend until
very finely chopped, scraping the mixture down from
the sides of the bowl if necessary. Tip into a shallow
ovenproof dish.

Scatter the prawns and fish over the fennel mixture,
and mix together a little. Scatter the peas on top.

Spoon half the cheese sauce over the filling, and
spread roughly with the back of a spoon. Layer the
potatoes on top, overlapping the slices and seasoning
each layer with salt and pepper as you go. Spoon the
remaining sauce over the top, spreading it in a thin layer.
Sprinkle with the cheese.

Bake in a preheated oven, 220°C (425°F), Gas Mark 7,
for 30 minutes until the surface has turned pale golden.
Reduce the oven temperature to 180°C (350°F), Gas
Mark 4, and cook for a further 30–40 minutes until the
potatoes are completely tender and the fish is cooked
through. Serve with a tomato salad.

For smoked fish & caper pie, use 625 g (1¼ lb)
smoked pollack fillets, skinned and cut into small
chunks, instead of the prawns and white fish. Replace
the green peppercorns with 2 tablespoons rinsed and
drained salted capers and follow the recipe as above.

chilli con carne

Serves **4**
Preparation time **5 minutes**
Cooking time **about 1 hour**

2 tablespoons **vegetable oil**
2 **onions**, chopped
1 **red pepper**, cored,
   deseeded and cut into cubes
2 **garlic cloves**, crushed
500 g (1 lb) **minced beef**
450 ml (¾ pint) **beef stock**
½–1 teaspoon **chilli powder**
475 g (15 oz) **canned red
   kidney beans**, drained
400 g (13 oz) can **chopped
   tomatoes**
1 tablespoon **tomato purée**
1 teaspoon **ground cumin**
salt and **pepper**
250 g (8 oz) **long-grain
   white rice**

To serve
soured cream
red chilli flakes
Cheddar cheese, grated
finely chopped **spring onion**

Heat the oil in a saucepan over a low heat. Add the onions and red pepper and gently fry, stirring now and then, for about 5 minutes until soft. Add the garlic and cook for another 1 minute until opaque.

Increase the heat slightly and add the meat. Fry until just brown, stirring and breaking up the meat with a wooden spoon. Pour in the stock, then add the chilli powder, beans, tomatoes, tomato purée, cumin and a dash of salt and pepper.

Bring to the boil, then cover, reduce the heat to as low as possible and simmer very gently for 50–60 minutes, stirring occasionally so that it does not stick to the bottom of the pan.

Cook the rice, towards the end of the chilli's cooking time, in lightly salted water, according to the packet instructions, then drain.

Pile up the rice on each of 4 warm serving plates, dollop on the cooked chilli and top with the soured cream. Scatter over the chilli flakes, grated Cheddar and spring onion and serve immediately with the boiled rice.

For veggie con carne, heat the oil in a pan, add the onion, red pepper and garlic as above, plus 1 diced aubergine. Fry, stirring, until softened, then add 2 diced courgettes and fry for a few minutes more, omitting the minced beef. Add the stock and remaining ingredients, and cook as above.

chicken kiev

Serves **4**
Preparation time **40 minutes**,
   plus freezing and chilling
Cooking time **20 minutes**

125 g (4 oz) **butter**, at room
   temperature
2 tablespoons chopped
   chives
1 tablespoon chopped **flat
   leaf parsley**
2 teaspoons chopped
   tarragon (optional)
1 **garlic clove**, finely chopped
2 teaspoons **lemon juice**
4 **boneless, skinless chicken
   breasts**, about 100 g (5 oz)
   each
2 tablespoons **plain flour**
125 g (4 oz) **fresh white
   breadcrumbs**
2 **eggs**
3 tablespoons **sunflower oil**
pepper

Beat the butter with the herbs, garlic, lemon juice and
a little pepper in a small bowl. Spoon into a line about
25 cm (10 inches) long on a sheet of clingfilm or foil,
then roll up into a neat log shape. Freeze for 15
minutes.

Meanwhile, put one of the chicken breasts between
two large sheets of clingfilm and beat with a meat
mallet or the side of a rolling pin until the chicken forms
a rectangle about 3 mm (1/8 inch) thick, being careful
not to make any holes. Repeat with the other chicken
breasts. Cut the herb butter log into 4 pieces and put
1 piece on each chicken breast. Fold in the sides of each
one, then the top and bottom, to make 4 tight parcels.

Put the flour on a plate and the breadcrumbs on a
second plate then whisk the eggs in a shallow dish.
Carefully roll the chicken parcels in the flour, then coat
in the egg and roll in the breadcrumbs. Put the coated
parcels back on to the empty flour plate and chill for
1 hour (longer if you have time).

Heat the oil in a large frying pan over a medium heat.
Add the chicken Kievs and fry for 5 minutes, turning
until evenly browned. Transfer to a baking sheet, then
complete cooking in a preheated oven, 200°C (400°F),
Gas Mark 6, for 15 minutes or until the chicken is
cooked through. Serve with braised red cabbage.

For chicken, garlic & sun-dried tomato Kievs, chop
50 g (2 oz) drained sun-dried tomatoes in oil and stir
into 150 g (5 oz) garlic and herb cream cheese. Divide
between the flattened chicken breasts, then shape, chill
and cook as above.

vegetable lasagne

Serves **4**
Preparation time **10 minutes**
Cooking time **1¼ hours**,
   plus standing

2 tablespoons **vegetable oil**
150 g (5 oz) **French beans**,
   chopped
1 **onion**, thinly sliced
400 g (13 oz) can **chopped
   tomatoes**
125 g (4 oz) **split red lentils**,
   picked over, rinsed
   and drained
300 ml (½ pint) **water**
pinch of **dried oregano**
500 g (1 lb) **cream cheese**
2 **eggs**, beaten
125 g (4 oz) **ready-cooked
   lasagne sheets**
2 tablespoons freshly grated
   Parmesan cheese
salt and **pepper**

Heat the oil in a saucepan over a low heat and fry the beans and onion for 5 minutes until the onion is soft and translucent.

Sprinkle with salt and pepper, then add the tomatoes, lentils, measurement water and oregano. Bring to the boil. Simmer for about 30 minutes or until the lentils are tender but not mushy. Mix together the cream cheese and beaten eggs in a bowl.

Spread half the vegetable and lentil mixture over the bottom of a large ovenproof dish, then cover with a third of the lasagne sheets. Pour over half the cheese mixture, then cover with another layer of lasagne sheets. Make a layer with the remaining vegetable and lentil mixture, cover with the remaining lasagne sheets and, finally, with the rest of the cheese mixture.

Sprinkle over the Parmesan and bake in a preheated oven, 180°C (350°F), Gas Mark 4, for 40 minutes. Remove from the oven and leave to stand for 5 minutes before cutting into slices and serving.

For beef lasagne, fry the sliced onion in the oil for 5 minutes until soft, omitting the French beans. Increase the heat slightly and add 500 g (1 lb) minced beef. Cook, stirring and breaking up the meat with a wooden spoon, until the mince is browned. Stir in 2 chopped garlic cloves, ½ teaspoon dried oregano and 1 tablespoon plain flour, then mix in the chopped tomatoes and 200 ml (7 fl oz) beef stock. Simmer gently for 45 minutes, stirring now and then, until the meat is tender. Layer in an ovenproof dish with the lasagne and cream cheese mixture and cook as above.

simple vegetable biriyani

Serves **4**
Preparation time **25 minutes**
Cooking time **about 1 hour**,
  plus standing

250 g (8 oz) **basmati rice**
6 tablespoons **vegetable oil**
2 large **onions**, sliced
2 teaspoons grated peeled
  fresh root ginger
2 **garlic cloves**, crushed
250 g (8 oz) **sweet potatoes**,
  peeled and cut into cubes
2 large **carrots**, cut into cubes
1 tablespoon **curry paste**
2 teaspoons **ground turmeric**
1 teaspoon **ground cinnamon**
1 teaspoon **chilli powder**
300 ml (½ pint) **vegetable
  stock**
4 **tomatoes**, skinned,
  deseeded and cubed
175 g (6 oz) **cauliflower
  florets**
125 g (4 oz) **frozen green
  peas**, thawed (optional)
50 g (2 oz) **cashew nuts**
2 **hard-boiled eggs**, peeled
  and cut into quarters
salt and **pepper**

Cook the rice in a saucepan of boiling water for 5 minutes. Drain in a colander, run under cold water, then drain again. Spread out the rice on a plate so that it dries out a little.

Heat 2 tablespoons of the oil in a frying pan over a medium heat. Add half the onion and fry for 10 minutes until very crisp and golden. Remove and set aside to drain on kitchen paper. Add the rest of the oil to the frying pan, and fry the rest of the onion and ginger for 5 minutes until the onion is soft and translucent, adding the garlic for the last minute of the cooking time. Add the sweet potatoes, carrots, curry paste and spices and fry for another 10 minutes until light golden.

Pour in the stock and add the tomatoes. Bring to the boil, reduce the heat, cover and simmer for 20 minutes. Add the cauliflower and peas, if liked, and cook for 8–10 minutes until the vegetables are tender. Check the seasoning and add salt and pepper if needed.

Mix in the rice and cashew nuts. Cook, stirring, for 3 minutes, then cover and remove from the heat. Leave to stand for 5 minutes, then serve sprinkled with the crispy-fried onions and topped with the hard-boiled eggs.

For chicken biryani, cook the rice and fry the onions for topping as above. Fry 500 g (1 lb) diced boneless, skinless chicken breasts in the remaining oil with the diced carrots, curry paste and spices for 10 minutes, stirring until golden. Add the stock and tomatoes and cook as above, adding 125 g (4 oz) frozen green peas instead of the cauliflower. Cook for 5 minutes. Stir in the rice and cashew nuts. Serve with the crispy-fried onion and egg as above.

roast lamb with wine & juniper

Serves **6**

Preparation time **20 minutes**

Cooking time **1 hour 35 minutes**

2 tablespoons **olive oil**

1 **leg of lamb**, about 1.5 kg (3 lb), trimmed of excess fat

10 **juniper berries**, crushed

3 **garlic cloves**, crushed

50 g (2 oz) **salted anchovies**, boned and rinsed

1 tablespoon **chopped rosemary**

2 tablespoons **balsamic vinegar**

2 sprigs of **rosemary**

300 ml (½ pint) **dry white wine**

salt and **pepper**

Heat the oil in a roasting tin in which the lamb will fit snugly over a medium-high heat. Add the lamb and cook until browned all over. Leave to cool.

Pound 6 of the juniper berries, the garlic, anchovies and chopped rosemary with the end of a rolling pin in a bowl, or use a mortar and pestle. Stir in the vinegar and mix to a paste.

Make small incisions all over the lamb with a small, sharp knife. Spread the paste over the lamb, working it into the incisions. Season with salt and pepper. Put the rosemary sprigs in the roasting tin and sit the lamb on top. Pour in the white wine and add the remaining white juniper.

Cover the roasting tin with foil and bring to the boil on the hob, then cook in a preheated oven, 160°C (325°F), Gas Mark 3, for 1 hour, turning the lamb every 20 minutes. Raise the temperature to 200°C (400°F), Gas Mark 6, remove the foil and roast for a further 30 minutes until the lamb is very tender. Serve with roast potatoes and steamed vegetables.

For leg of lamb with lemon & rosemary, omit the juniper berries and pound the grated rind of 2 lemons with the garlic, anchovies and chopped rosemary. Replace the vinegar with 4 tablespoons lemon juice. Spoon the paste over the lamb, working it into the incisions as above, and continue with the rest of the recipe.

traditional roast turkey

Serves **8**

Preparation time **45 minutes**, plus resting

Cooking time **3 hours 40 minutes**

5 kg (10 lb) **turkey**, giblets removed and cavity rinsed

1 packet **ready-made stuffing**

1 tablespoon **dried basil**

paprika, for sprinkling

50 g (2 oz) **butter**

6 **streaky bacon rashers** (optional)

1 **lemon**, sliced

1 **orange**, sliced

salt and **pepper**

Gravy

600 ml (1 pint) **chicken** or **vegetable stock**

90 ml (3 fl oz) **port** or **white wine**

1 tablespoon **cornflour**

If using a frozen bird, make sure that the turkey is completely thawed before using. Take the turkey out of the refrigerator a couple of hours before you intend to start cooking, to allow it to come to room temperature.

Put the turkey in a large roasting tin, make up the stuffing as packet instructions and use to stuff the neck of the bird. Sprinkle the turkey with the basil and paprika and season. Lay the bacon rashers over the breast, if using, and tuck the lemon and orange slices around it. Loosely cover with foil, tucking the edges in around the edge of the roasting tin. Roast in a preheated oven, 180°C (350°F), Gas Mark 4, for 20 minutes per 500 g (1 lb) plus 20 minutes. Baste regularly.

Remove the foil 20 minutes before the end so that the turkey browns. Transfer the turkey to a warm serving dish, cover with foil and leave to rest while you make the gravy. Skim off and discard the fat from the pan juices, then pour in the stock and port or wine and bring to the boil. Stir in cornflour and some cold water to thicken the gravy. Carve the turkey and eat with roast potatoes, carrots and vegetables of your choice.

For crispy roast potatoes, to accompany the turkey, peel and cut 1.5 kg (3 lb) potatoes into chunky pieces. Add to a saucepan of salted boiling water and cook for 8–10 minutes until the edges are just breaking up. Drain well, return to the pan and shake. Heat 5 tablespoons sunflower oil or goose fat in a roasting tin on the shelf above the turkey for 2–3 minutes until very hot. Carefully add the potatoes to the tin, spooning the oil or fat on top. Roast in the oven for 1 hour, turning once or twice, until golden. Drain off the oil or fat and serve with the turkey.

comfort food & snacks

garlic bread

Serves **2**
Preparation time **5 minutes**
Cooking time **4 minutes**

4 slices of **bread** such as
    ciabatta, sourdough, French
    bread or pitta
2–3 **garlic cloves**, peeled
    and halved
125 ml (4 fl oz) **olive oil**
a little chopped **flat leaf
    parsley** (optional)
salt

Toast the bread on both sides under a preheated
medium grill until golden. While the bread is still
warm, rub one side with the cut sides of the garlic.

Put the warm toasted bread on a plate and drizzle
2 tablespoons of the olive oil over each slice. Sprinkle
with salt and a little chopped parsley, if liked, and serve
as a starter, snack or with any pasta dish or salad.

For tomato & basil bread, toast the bread as
above and rub with the garlic, then mix the oil with
2 teaspoons sun-dried tomato purée (from a tube)
and 2 tablespoons chopped basil. Drizzle over the
toasted bread, then serve.

poached eggs, bacon & muffins

Serves **4**
Preparation time **5 minutes**
Cooking time **about**
   20 minutes

4 ripe **tomatoes**, thickly sliced
2 tablespoons chopped **basil**
2 tablespoons **olive oil**
8 **back** or **streaky bacon**
   rashers
4 split and toasted **English**
   muffins, buttered, or 4
   slices toasted **bread** such as
   ciabatta, buttered, to serve
4 large **eggs**
1 tablespoon **vinegar**
salt and **pepper**

Lay the tomato slices in a grill pan. Mix together the basil and oil in a bowl, then drizzle over the tomatoes. Season with lots of salt and pepper. Cook under a preheated medium grill for 3–4 minutes until starting to soften. Arrange the bacon rashers on top of the tomatoes and grill for 6–8 minutes, turning once.

Poach the eggs, by breaking 1 of the eggs into a ramekin or cup, making sure not to break the yolk. Bring a large saucepan of water to the boil. Add the vinegar to the boiling water, then stir the water rapidly in a circular motion to make a whirlpool. Carefully slide the egg into the centre of the pan while the water is still swirling, holding the ramekin or cup as close to the water as you can. Repeat with the other eggs and cook for 3 minutes. Lift the poached eggs out with a slotted spoon.

Put a hot buttered muffin or slice of toasted bread on a warm plate. Top half of the muffin or the toast with grilled tomatoes and 2 rashers of bacon, then put the poached egg on top. Cook and serve the other 3 eggs in the same way, swirling the boiling water into a whirlpool each time before sliding in the egg. (Poaching the eggs separately ensures each serving is as fresh and hot as possible at the table.) Serve.

For poached eggs with mushrooms, omit the tomatoes, herbs and bacon. Heat 2 tablespoons olive oil in a frying pan, add 200 g (7 oz) trimmed sliced closed-cup white or chestnut mushrooms. Sauté, stirring, for a few minutes until softened and golden. Add 1 tablespoon Worcestershire sauce and 1 tablespoon ketchup and stir through. Spoon over toasted and buttered muffins and top each with a poached egg.

baked tortillas with hummus

Serves **4**
Preparation time **5 minutes**
Cooking time **10–12 minutes**

4 small **soft flour tortillas**
1 tablespoon **olive oil**

Hummus
400 g (13 oz) can **chickpeas**,
  drained and rinsed
1 **garlic clove**, chopped
4 tablespoons **Greek-style
  yogurt**
2 tablespoons **lemon juice**
2 **garlic cloves**, peeled and
  finely chopped
1 small bunch **fresh
  coriander**, chopped
salt and **pepper**
paprika, for sprinkling

Make the hummus first. Put the chickpeas in a bowl, and mash with a fork to break them up. Add the garlic, yogurt, lemon juice and coriander and season with salt and pepper. Mix together. Alternatively, put all the ingredients except the coriander in a blender or food processor and blend to a coarse purée. Add the coriander and whiz briefly until mixed through. Put the hummus in a serving bowl or dish and sprinkle with a little paprika.

Cut each tortilla into 8 triangles, put on a baking sheet and brush with a little oil. Bake in a preheated oven, 200°C (400°F), Gas Mark 6, for 10–12 minutes until golden and crisp. Remove from the oven.

Serve the tortilla triangles with the hummus for dipping or spreading on top.

For baked tortillas with broad bean hummus, cook 400 g (13 oz) frozen broad beans in boiling water for 4–5 minutes until tender. Drain, then mash or purée with the garlic, yogurt, lemon juice, salt and pepper as above. Mix in 3 tablespoons chopped mint leaves, 1 chopped deseeded fresh green chilli and 1 teaspoon ground cumin instead of the fresh coriander.

macaroni & haddock cheese

Serves **4**
Preparation time **2 minutes**
Cooking time **30 minutes**

600 ml (1 pint) **milk**
325 g (11 oz) **undyed smoked haddock fillets**
325 g (11 oz) **dried macaroni**
50 g (2 oz) **unsalted butter**
25 g (1 oz) **plain flour**
1 tablespoon **wholegrain mustard**
250 ml (8 fl oz) **single cream**
125 g (4 oz) **shelled green peas**, thawed if frozen
125 g (4 oz) **Cheddar cheese**, grated
4 tablespoons freshly grated **Parmesan cheese**
1 tablespoon roughly chopped **flat leaf parsley**
125 g (4 oz) **fresh white** or **wholemeal breadcrumbs**
1 tablespoon **olive oil**
salt and **pepper**

Heat the milk to scalding point (just before boiling point) in a wide-based shallow saucepan. Add the haddock, in a single layer, and poach gently for 6–8 minutes until the flesh flakes easily. Lift the fish from the pan with a slotted spoon. Once the fish is cool enough to handle, remove and discard the skin and break the flesh into large flakes. Strain the milk in which the fish was cooked into a jug and set aside.

Cook the pasta in a large saucepan of salted boiling water until al dente. Meanwhile, melt the butter in a saucepan over a very low heat. Sprinkle in the flour and cook, stirring with a wooden spoon, for 2 minutes until the mixture is a light biscuity colour. Remove the pan from the heat and slowly add the reserved milk, stirring away lumps. Return the pan to the heat and simmer, stirring, for 2–3 minutes until thickened and creamy. Stir in the mustard, cream, peas, Cheddar and half the Parmesan. Season with salt and pepper.

Drain the pasta and return to the pan. Fold the cheese sauce and haddock flakes into the pasta, then transfer to a greased ovenproof dish. Mix the parsley and remaining Parmesan into the breadcrumbs, then scatter evenly over the pasta. Drizzle with the oil and bake in a preheated oven, 220°C (425°F), Gas Mark 7, for 10 minutes until bubbling and golden.

For tarragon carrots, to serve as a side dish, blanch 250–300 g (8–10 oz) halved baby carrots in boiling water for 2 minutes. Drain and return to the pan. Cook gently, with the lid on, in 25 g (1 oz) butter, 1 tablespoon olive oil and 1 teaspoon sugar for 5 minutes until tender. Add 2 tablespoons chopped tarragon before serving.

sausages with mustard mash

Serves **4**
Preparation time **5 minutes**
Cooking time **25 minutes**

8 good-quality **thick pork** or
   beef sausages
2 **onions**, cut into wedges

Mustard mash

1 kg (2 lb) **floury potatoes**
   such as Maris Piper, King
   Edward or Desiree, scrubbed
   and quartered (leave
   unpeeled)
75 g (3 oz) **butter**
1–2 tablespoons **smooth**
   Dijon mustard
1 **garlic clove**, crushed
1 large bunch of **flat leaf**
   parsley, chopped
dash of **olive oil**
salt and **pepper**

Start the mustard mash first. Put the potatoes in a large saucepan of cold water, bring to the boil and simmer for 15 minutes until tender.

Grill the sausages, meanwhile, in a frying pan over a medium heat or under a preheated medium grill for 10 minutes, turning to get an even colour. Add the onion wedges and cook with the sausages for 6–7 minutes until softened and starting to colour.

Drain the potatoes well when they are cooked. Once they are cool enough to handle, peel them and return to the pan. Mash well, so that they are nice and creamy.

Add the butter, mustard, garlic and a good sprinkling of salt and pepper, and carry on mashing. Taste and add more mustard, if liked. Finally, stir in the parsley and a dash of olive oil.

Pile up a serving of the mash on each of 4 warm plates and stick the sausages and onion wedges on top. Serve immediately with gravy for pouring over (see below).

For caramelized onion gravy, to accompany the sausages, heat 1 tablespoon sunflower oil in a frying pan over low heat, add 1 large thinly sliced onion and fry gently for 10 minutes until just starting to colour. Sprinkle over 1 teaspoon caster sugar and cook for 5 minutes more, stirring until caramelized and browned. Stir in 1 tablespoon plain flour and cook for a minute or so. Pour in 250 ml (8 fl oz) beef stock and season with salt and pepper. Stir through. Simmer for 5 minutes, stirring frequently. Serve hot.

falafel burgers

Serves **4**
Preparation time **15 minutes**,
   plus chilling
Cooking time **8 minutes**

425 g (14 oz) can **chickpeas**,
   drained and rinsed
2 **garlic cloves**, crushed
1 **small red onion**, finely
   chopped
2 teaspoons **ground cumin**
2 tablespoons chopped **fresh
   coriander**
2 tablespoons chopped **flat
   leaf parsley**
grated rind of 1 **lemon**
1 **egg yolk**
2 tablespoons **gram (besan)**
   or **plain flour**
vegetable oil for frying
salt and **pepper**

Garlic and mint sauce
200 ml (7 fl oz) **natural** or
   thick Greek yogurt
2 tablespoons **chopped mint**
1 **garlic clove**, crushed

To serve
8 mini **pitta breads**
6 tablespoons ready-made **red
   pepper** or ordinary **hummus**

Put all the ingredients for the falafel, except the flour
and oil, in the bowl of a food processor. Season with
salt and pepper, then process into a rough paste. Using
slightly wet hands, divide the mixture into 8 equal-sized
balls, flattening them a little to make burgers. Cover and
chill for 30 minutes.

Mix together the yogurt, mint and garlic in a small bowl.
Season with salt and pepper, and set aside until needed.

Coat the chilled falafel burgers lightly with the gram or
plain flour. Pour just enough oil for shallow-frying into
a heavy frying pan over a medium-high heat. When the
oil is hot, carefully add the falafel burgers and fry for
4 minutes on each side until golden brown and crisp.

Toast the pitta breads under a preheated hot grill until
warmed through but still soft. Spread each one with
some hummus and top with the salad and a burger.
Sprinkle with a little paprika, and serve immediately
with the garlic mint sauce for spooning over the top.

southern fried chicken

Serves **4**

Preparation time **25 minutes**

Cooking time **40–45 minutes**

6 tablespoons **sunflower oil**

1½ teaspoons **smoked paprika**

1½ teaspoons **dried oregano**

1 teaspoon **dried mustard powder**

1 teaspoon **crushed chillies**

500 g (1 lb) **sweet potatoes**, peeled and cut into thick wedges

500 g (1 lb) **floury potatoes** such as Maris Piper or King Edward, scrubbed and cut into thick wedges

4 tablespoons **plain flour**

2 **eggs**

2 tablespoons **water**

125 g (4 oz) **fresh white breadcrumbs**

4 **chicken legs** (thighs with drumsticks attached)

salt and **pepper**

Mix together 3 tablespoons of the oil, 1 teaspoon of the paprika, 1 teaspoon of the oregano, ½ teaspoon of the mustard, ½ teaspoon of the crushed chillies and some salt in a large bowl. Add the potatoes and toss in the oil mixture until coated.

Put the flour on a large plate and mix through the remaining paprika, oregano, mustard, crushed chillies and season. Whisk together the eggs and water in a shallow dish and put the breadcrumbs on a large plate. Coat the chicken in the flour mixture, then beaten egg, then breadcrumbs, until covered.

Heat a large roasting tin in a preheated oven, 200°C (400°F), Gas Mark 6, for 5 minutes. Meanwhile, heat the remaining oil in a large frying pan, add the chicken and fry on all sides for about 10 minutes until pale golden; do not be tempted to fry for too long because the chicken browns further in the oven. Transfer the chicken to the hot roasting tin, add the potato wedges and roast for 30–35 minutes until the chicken is cooked through and the potatoes are crisp and golden. Transfer to 4 warm plates and serve with mayonnaise and salad.

For cheesy fried chicken escalopes, make up the potato wedges as above, then mix the remaining paprika, crushed chillies and a little salt and pepper with the flour. Take 4 boneless, skinless chicken breasts, about 125 g (4 oz) each, and using a sharp knife cut horizontally into thin, flat slices about 5 mm (¼ inches) thick. Coat in the flour mixture, then the beaten egg, then in 100 g (3½ oz) fresh white breadcrumbs mixed with 2 tablespoons freshly grated Parmesan cheese. Fry in the oil for 10–12 minutes until golden and cooked.

spinach & potato gratin

Serves **4**

Preparation time **10 minutes**

Cooking time **35 minutes**

625 g (1 ¼ lb) **potatoes**, peeled and thinly sliced

500 g (1 lb) **spinach leaves**

200 g (7 oz) **mozzarella cheese**, grated

4 **tomatoes**, sliced

3 **eggs**, beaten

300 ml (½ pint) **whipping cream**

salt and **pepper**

Cook the potato slices in a large saucepan of salted boiling water for 5 minutes, then drain well.

Cook the spinach, meanwhile, in a separate saucepan of boiling water for 1–2 minutes until just wilted. Drain in a colander, then squeeze out the excess water.

Grease a large ovenproof dish and line the bottom with half the potato slices. Cover with the spinach and half the mozzarella, seasoning each layer well with salt and pepper. Cover with the remaining potato slices and arrange the tomato slices on top. Sprinkle with the remaining mozzarella.

Whisk together the eggs and cream in a bowl and season well with salt and pepper. Pour over the ingredients in the dish.

Bake in a preheated oven, 180°C (350°F), Gas Mark 4, for about 30 minutes until bubbling and golden. Serve immediately with a salad and crusty bread.

For tomato, lime & basil salad, to serve as an accompaniment, slice or quarter 1 kg (2 lb) tomatoes while the gratin is baking and arrange in a large serving bowl. Scatter over ½ red onion, thinly sliced, and a handful of basil leaves. Whisk together 4 tablespoons olive oil, 2 tablespoons chopped basil, 1 tablespoon lime juice, 1 teaspoon grated lime rind, ½ teaspoon clear honey, 1 crushed garlic clove and a pinch of cayenne pepper. Season with salt and pepper. Whisk again and pour over the salad. Cover and leave to stand at room temperature for about 30 minutes, to allow the flavours to mingle. Serve with the gratin.

cod rarebit

Serves **4**

Preparation time **5 minutes**

Cooking time **15 minutes**

2 tablespoons **wholegrain mustard**

3 tablespoons **beer** or **milk**

250 g (8 oz) **Cheddar cheese**, grated

2 tablespoons **olive oil**

4 pieces of **cod fillet**, about 200 g (7 oz) each, pin-boned

salt and **pepper**

Mix together the mustard, beer or milk and cheese in a small saucepan. Allow the cheese to melt over a low heat. Stir occasionally and do not allow the mixture to boil, as the cheese will curdle. Remove the pan from the heat and leave to cool and thicken.

Put the oil in a frying pan over a high heat. Season the fish with salt and pepper, then carefully place into the pan, skin side down. Pan-fry for 4–5 minutes until the skin is crispy, then turn the fish over and cook for a further minute on the other side until the fish is cooked through; be careful not to overcook.

Spread the cooled cheese sauce over the fish, and slide the pan under a preheated grill (keeping the handle away from the heat). Grill for a minute or so until the cheese sauce is bubbling and golden brown.

For wholegrain mustard & cream sauce, to serve as an accompaniment to the pan-fried cod instead of the rarebit topping, put 2 finely chopped shallots, 1 crushed garlic clove and a little olive oil in a small saucepan over a low heat. Gently sweat the shallots and garlic for a few minutes until soft and translucent. Pour in 100 ml (3½ fl oz) chicken stock and 200 ml (7 fl oz) double cream, and bring to the boil. Stir in 1 tablespoon wholegrain mustard and serve hot poured over the pan-fried cod.

toad in the hole

Serves **4**
Preparation time **10 minutes**
Cooking time **25 minutes**

125 g (4 oz) **plain flour**
1 **egg**
300 ml (½ pint) **milk** or equal
   mixture of **milk** and **water**
500 g (1 lb) good-quality **pork**
   sausages
8 **rindless bacon rashers**
2 tablespoons **vegetable oil**
salt and **pepper**

Put the flour and a dash of salt and pepper in a bowl, then crack in the egg. Slowly whisk in the milk or milk-and-water mixture until the batter is smooth and frothy.

Separate the sausages from each other. Stretch each rasher of bacon by laying it on a chopping board and running the flat edge of a knife along the rasher until it is half as long again. Wrap a rasher of bacon around each sausage.

Pour the oil into a roasting tin and add the bacon-wrapped sausages, keeping them spaced apart. Roast in a preheated oven, 220°C (425°F), Gas Mark 7, for 5 minutes until sizzling. Whisk the batter again.

Take the roasting tin out of the oven and quickly pour in the batter, making sure that the sausages are still spaced apart. Return the tin to the oven and cook for about 20 minutes until the batter is risen and golden and the sausages are cooked through. Delicious with baked beans and mashed potatoes.

For vegetarian toad in the hole, make up the batter as above, adding a large pinch of dried mixed herbs. Cook 8 vegetarian sausages and 2 small red onions, cut into wedges, in 2 tablespoons hot oil in the roasting tin as above. Pour over the batter and continue as above.

vegetable samosas

Makes **12**
Preparation time **10 minutes**
Cooking time **15–20 minutes**

3 large **potatoes**, boiled,
   peeled and roughly mashed
100 g (3½ oz) **cooked green
   peas**
1 teaspoon **cumin seeds**
1 teaspoon **amchoor** (dried
   mango powder)
2 **fresh green chillies**,
   deseeded and finely
   chopped
1 small **red onion**, finely
   chopped
3 tablespoons chopped **fresh
   coriander leaves**
1 tablespoon **mint**, chopped
4 tablespoons **lemon juice**
12 **filo pastry sheets**,
   about 30 x 18 cm
   (12 x 7 inches) each
75 g (3 oz) **butter**, melted, for
   brushing
salt and **pepper**

Mix together the potatoes, peas, cumin seeds, amchoor, chillies, onion, coriander, mint and lemon juice in a large bowl. Add a dash of salt and pepper.

Fold each sheet of filo pastry in half lengthways. It is best to work with 1 sheet of filo at a time; keep the other sheets covered with a slightly damp tea towel or clingfilm while you work, to prevent them from drying out. Brush the first pastry sheet with a little melted butter. Put a large spoonful of the potato mixture at one end, then fold the corner of the pastry over the mixture, covering it to make a triangular shape. Brush with a little more butter if needed. Continue folding over the triangle of pastry along the length of the pastry strip to make a neat triangular samosa.

Make 11 more samosas in the same way, dividing the mixture evenly and brushing the pastry with a little melted butter as you go.

Arrange the samosas side by side on a baking sheet, brush with melted butter and bake in a preheated oven, 200°C (400°F), Gas Mark 6, for 15–20 minutes until golden. Serve hot.

burritos with pork stuffing

Serves **4**
Preparation time **20 minutes**
Cooking time **90 minutes**,
  plus resting

1 kg (2 lb) **boneless rolled
  pork shoulder**
1 tablespoon **vegetable oil**
350 ml (12 fl oz) **chicken
  stock**
4 tablespoons **tomato purée**
½ teaspoon grated **orange
  rind**
1 teaspoon **dried red chilli
  flakes**
8 **soft flour tortillas**
salt

Topping
soured cream
½ **avocado**, halved, stoned,
  peeled and chopped
1 teaspoon **dried red chilli
  flakes**

Put the pork in a roasting tin and brush with a little oil.
Sprinkle with salt and roast in a preheated oven, 200°C
(400°F), Gas Mark 6, for 30 minutes. Reduce the oven
temperature to 180°C (350°F), Gas Mark 4, and roast
for another 1 hour or until crisp and golden. Test to
make sure that the pork is cooked through by inserting
a skewer into the meat – the juices should run clear. Set
aside in a warm place, covered with foil, for 15 minutes.

Make the sauce, meanwhile. Pour the stock into a
saucepan. Add the tomato purée, orange rind and
chilli flakes. Bring to the boil, then reduce the heat and
simmer for about 30 minutes until the sauce is thick.

Take off the crackling from the roast pork using a sharp
knife and cut into strips. Next, cut away any fat on the
pork and discard. Tear the meat into shreds. Add the
shredded pork to the sauce and heat over low heat.

Pop the tortillas in the oven for a couple of minutes to
warm and soften (don't let them become dried out and
crisp, or you will not be able to roll them properly). Put
a little of the pork mixture in the centre of each warm
tortilla and roll them up. Dollop soured cream on top of
the burritos, then pile on the avocado and sprinkle chilli
flakes over the top. Serve with the crackling, if you wish.

For speedy burritos with chicken stuffing, make the
sauce as above. While this reduces down, thinly slice
625 g (1¼ lb) boneless, skinless chicken breasts. Fry in
2 tablespoons vegetable oil for 10 minutes, turning until
golden. Add to the tomato sauce for the last 10 minutes
of cooking. Serve with wraps, cream and avocado.

onion rings in beer batter

Serves **4**

Preparation time **10 minutes**

Cooking time **10 minutes**

4 large **onions**

vegetable oil, for deep-frying

Batter

1 **egg**, separated

1 tablespoon **olive oil**

100 ml (3½ fl oz) **light beer**
  such as lager, chilled

65 g (2½ oz) **plain flour**

salt and **pepper**

Slice the onions into 5 mm (¼ inch) thick rings and separate out. Keep the larger rings and ditch the rest, or keep to fry up the next day for breakfast.

Make the batter next. Whisk together the egg yolk, oil, beer and flour in a bowl. Season with salt and pepper. In another clean, dry bowl, whisk the egg white until stiff, then gently fold into the batter until smooth and combined.

Heat 5 cm (2 inches) of vegetable oil in a deep heavy-based saucepan or a deep-fat fryer to 180°–190°C (350°–375°F), or until a cube of bread dropped into the oil browns in 30 seconds.

Dip the onion rings, a few at a time, into the batter, then carefully drop into the oil and deep-fry in batches for 1–2 minutes until golden. Remove very carefully using a slotted spoon and drain on kitchen paper. Serve at once with mayonnaise, while the onions are crisp and piping hot.

For mushrooms in beer batter, wipe 500 g (1 lb) button mushrooms with kitchen paper and dip in the batter. Deep-fry as above, then serve immediately with 150 ml (¼ pint) mayonnaise flavoured with 2 chopped garlic cloves.

minty lamb kebabs

Serves **4**
Preparation time **10 minutes**,
    plus marinating and soaking
Cooking time **8–10 minutes**

150 ml (¼ pint) **low-fat
    natural yogurt**
1 **garlic clove**, crushed
2 tablespoons chopped **mint**
1 tablespoon **mint sauce**
350 g (12 oz) **lean boneless
    lamb**, cubed
2 small **red** or **white onions**,
    cut into wedges
1 **green pepper**, cored,
    deseeded and cut into
    wedges

To serve
green salad
couscous
lemon wedges (optional)

Soak 8 wooden skewers in cold water for at least
30 minutes, to prevent them burning while the kebabs
are cooking; if using metal skewers, you can leave
out this step, of course.

Mix together the yogurt, garlic, mint and mint sauce in
a bowl. Add the lamb and stir well. Cover and leave to
marinate in a cool place for 10 minutes or preferably
in the refrigerator for at least 1 hour, to allow the meat
to absorb more of the flavours.

Thread the lamb and onion and green pepper wedges
alternately on to the wooden or metal skewers (metal
skewers help the meat to cook right through), arrange
on a grill rack and cook under a preheated medium-
hot grill for 8–10 minutes, turning once, until the meat
is cooked through and the onions and peppers are
softened and starting to brown. Alternatively, grill the
skewers in a preheated griddle pan or over a barbecue.

Serve hot with green salad, couscous and lemon
wedges, if liked.

For curried lamb kebabs, mix the yogurt with
1 tablespoon mild curry paste, 1 tablespoon mango
chutney and 1 chopped garlic clove. Marinate the
lamb as above, thread on to the skewers alternately
with the onions and green pepper, grill as above and
serve with rice.

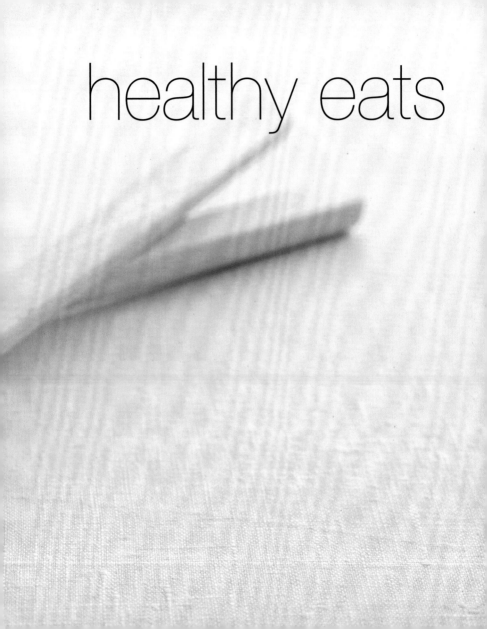

healthy eats

chorizo, pepper & oregano salad

Serves **2–4**
Preparation time **15 minutes**
Cooking time **15 minutes**

200 g (7 oz) **chorizo sausage**
1 tablespoon **olive oil**
2 **red peppers**, cored,
    deseeded and cut into 2 cm
    (¾ inch) squares
2 **yellow peppers**, cored,
    deseeded and cut into 2 cm
    (¾ inch) squares
1 **red onion**, finely diced
2 tablespoons **sherry vinegar**
½ bunch of **oregano**, roughly
    chopped
75 g (3 oz) **rocket**
salt and **pepper**

Peel off the outer wrapping, or 'skin', on the chorizo sausage. Cut the sausage into thick slices. Set aside.

Put the oil in a large frying pan over a high heat, add the red and yellow peppers and cook for 2–3 minutes until they start to colour. Add the chorizo and fry for another 3 minutes, then reduce the heat to low and add the onion. Cook for a further 3 minutes until the onion is soft and translucent.

Deglaze the pan with the sherry vinegar, scraping up any bits on the bottom with a wooden spoon, and reduce for 1 minute.

Transfer the contents of the pan to a large salad bowl and leave to cool slightly. Toss gently with the oregano and rocket. Season with salt and pepper and serve with Romesco Sauce (see below).

For romesco sauce, to serve as an accompaniment, soak 1 ancho chilli in a bowl of cold water for 1 hour; drain. Put the ancho chilli, 4 ready-marinated red peppers, 2 peeled and deseeded tomatoes, 20 g (¾ oz) blanched toasted almonds, 20 g (¾ oz) toasted hazelnuts, 1 garlic clove, 1 tablespoon red wine vinegar and 1 teaspoon smoked paprika into a food processor or blender. Whiz briefly to make a smooth sauce. Season with salt and pepper and serve with the salad.

spicy apple & potato soup

Serves **4**
Preparation time **15 minutes**
Cooking time **30 minutes**

50 g (2 oz) **butter**
1 small **onion**, chopped
2 **dessert apples**, peeled,
  cored and sliced
pinch of **cayenne pepper**
  (or to taste), plus extra
  for sprinkling
600 ml (1 pint) **vegetable
  stock**
300 g (10 oz) **floury potatoes**,
  sliced
300 ml (½ pint) **hot milk**
salt

Apple garnish
15 g (½ oz) **butter**
½–1 **dessert apple**, peeled,
  cored and diced

Melt the butter in a large heavy-based saucepan over a medium heat. Add the onion and cook for 5 minutes or until softened. Add the apples and cayenne and cook, stirring, for another 2 minutes.

Pour in the stock, then add the potatoes. Bring to the boil, then reduce the heat and simmer gently for 15–18 minutes until the apples and potatoes are very tender.

Blend the soup in batches in a blender or food processor until very smooth, then transfer to a clean saucepan. Reheat gently and stir in the hot milk. Taste and adjust the seasoning if necessary.

Make the apple garnish, meanwhile. Melt the butter in a small frying pan, add the diced apple and cook over a high heat until crisp.

Serve the soup in warm bowls, garnishing each portion with some diced apple and a sprinkling of cayenne.

For spicy apple & parsnip soup, fry the onion and apples as above, omitting the cayenne. Add ½ teaspoon ground turmeric and 1 teaspoon ground coriander and stir through to coat the apple and onion mixture in the spices. Pour in 600 ml (1 pint) chicken or vegetable stock, then add 300 g (10 oz) diced parsnips instead of the potatoes. Season with salt and black pepper. Continue the recipe as above.

prawn & borlotti salad

Serves **4**

Preparation time **15 minutes**, plus cooling

Cooking time **up to 30 minutes**

200 g (7 oz) shelled **fresh borlotti beans** (about 450 g/14½ oz in the pod) or 410 g (14 oz) can **borlotti beans**, rinsed and drained

2 tablespoons **extra virgin olive oil**

2 **garlic cloves**, crushed

1 **fresh red chilli**, deseeded and finely chopped

2 **celery sticks**, thinly sliced

200 g (7 oz) **cooked peeled prawns**, tails left on

grated rind and juice of 1 **lemon**

50 g (2 oz) **wild rocket**

salt

Tip the fresh borlotti beans, if using, into a saucepan. Add enough cold water to cover by about 5 cm (2 inches) and bring to the boil. Skim off any scum that rises to the surface, then reduce the heat to a simmer and cook, uncovered, for 30 minutes or until tender; drain. If using canned beans, simply rinse under cold running water before using, then heat gently in a saucepan over a medium heat for 3 minutes.

Put the oil, garlic and chilli in a large bowl. Stir in the warm beans and the celery and season with salt. Leave the salad to cool to room temperature. You can then cover and store in the refrigerator for up to 1 day.

Leave the beans to return to room temperature before serving if you have prepared them in advance. Stir in the prawns and lemon rind and juice, then gently toss through with the rocket or scatter on top. Serve at once.

For sardine, pea & borlotti salad, prepare and cool the borlotti beans as above, then toss with the lemon rind and juice, omitting the prawns and rocket. Add 2 x 120 g (3¾ oz) cans sardines in tomato sauce, a 5 cm (2 inch) piece of diced cucumber, 4 chopped spring onions and 100 g (3½ oz) just-cooked frozen peas and gently toss through. Serve on a bed of torn Little Gem lettuce or iceberg lettuce leaves.

malaysian coconut vegetables

Serves **4**

Preparation time **15 minutes**, plus soaking

Cooking time **20 minutes**

125 g (4 oz) **broccoli florets**

125 g (4 oz) **French beans**, cut into 2.5 cm (1 inch) lengths

1 **red pepper**, cored, deseeded and sliced

125 g (4 oz) **courgettes**, thinly sliced

Coconut sauce

25 g (1 oz) **tamarind pulp**

150 ml (¼ pint) **boiling water**

400 ml (14 fl oz) can **coconut milk**

2 teaspoons **Thai green curry paste**

1 teaspoon grated **fresh root ginger**

1 **onion**, cut into small cubes

½ teaspoon **ground turmeric**

salt

Make the coconut sauce. Put the tamarind in a bowl. Pour over the measurement water and leave to soak for 30 minutes. Mash the tamarind in the water, then push through a sieve set over another bowl, squashing the tamarind so that you get as much of the pulp as possible; discard the stringy bits and any seeds.

Take 2 tablespoons of the cream from the top of the coconut milk and pour it into a wok or large frying pan. Add the curry paste, ginger, onion and turmeric, and cook over a gentle heat, stirring, for 2–3 minutes. Stir in the rest of the coconut milk and the tamarind water. Bring to the boil, then reduce the heat to a simmer and add a pinch of salt.

Add the broccoli to the coconut sauce and cook for 5 minutes, then add the green beans and red pepper. Cook, stirring, for another 5 minutes. Finally, stir in the courgettes and cook gently for 1–2 minutes until the courgette is just tender. Serve immediately with some crispy prawn crackers.

For chicken & green beans in coconut sauce, soak the tamarind and make the coconut sauce as above. Add 500 g (1 lb) diced boneless, skinless chicken breast to the wok or frying pan. Simmer for 5 minutes, then add the sliced French beans, omitting the red pepper and courgettes. Simmer gently for another 5 minutes until the chicken is cooked through. Serve with noodles.

tuna with green beans & broccoli

Serves **4**
Preparation time **8 minutes**
Cooking time **15 minutes**

500 g (1 lb) **new potatoes**,
scrubbed
250 g (8 oz) **fine French
beans**, topped and tailed
200 g (7 oz) **tenderstem
broccoli**
4 **fresh tuna steaks**, about
175 g (6 oz) each
1 tablespoon **olive oil**
50 g (2 oz) **toasted
hazelnuts**, roughly chopped
salt and **pepper**

Dressing
4 tablespoons **hazelnut oil**
1 tablespoon **lemon juice**
1 teaspoon **Dijon mustard**

Cook the potatoes in a saucepan of lightly salted boiling water for 10–15 minutes (depending on the size of the potatoes) until just tender. Drain and leave to cool slightly.

Meanwhile cook the beans and broccoli in 2 separate pans of fresh lightly salted boiling water until tender, but still with a slight bite. The French beans will take 4–5 minutes and the broccoli about 3 minutes; be careful not to overcook. Drain the beans and broccoli as soon as they are ready, then tip immediately into ice-cold water to stop the cooking process. Drain again. Cut the cooled potatoes into quarters lengthways. Set aside.

Whisk together all the dressing ingredients in a small bowl (or put them in a screw-top jar with a tight-fitting lid and shake vigorously) and season.

Heat a griddle pan over a very high heat. Season the tuna steaks with salt and pepper, and rub with the olive oil. Carefully place in the pan and sear for 1 minute on each side (or longer if the steaks are thickly cut or you want your tuna cooked through, rather than pink).

Put the potatoes, beans and broccoli in a large bowl or serving dish. Add the dressing and toss through gently. Sprinkle with the hazelnuts and serve with the tuna.

For Asian green beans, to serve as an alternative accompaniment, mix together 1 tablespoon sesame oil, 2 teaspoons light soy sauce, 1 deseeded and finely chopped fresh red chilli, 1 teaspoon clear honey and 1 tablespoon chopped fresh coriander. Cook 500 g (1 lb) topped and tailed French beans in salted boiling water as above. Drain and, while warm, toss in the dressing.

griddled summer chicken salad

Serves **4**

Preparation time **15 minutes**

Cooking time **45 minutes**

4 **boneless, skinless chicken
  breasts**, about 125 g
  (4 oz) each
2 small **red onions**
2 **red peppers**, cored,
  deseeded and cut into flat
  pieces
1 bunch of **fresh asparagus**,
  trimmed
200 g (7 oz) **new potatoes**,
  scrubbed, boiled until tender
  and halved lengthways
1 bunch of **basil**
75 ml (3 fl oz) **olive oil**
2 tablespoons **balsamic
  vinegar**
salt and **pepper**

Heat a griddle pan (or ordinary frying pan) over a medium-high heat. Place the chicken breasts in the pan and cook for 8–10 minutes on each side. If you are using a griddle pan, cook the chicken on each side without moving it in the pan, so that it ends up with a distinct striped pattern; if you like, change the position of the chicken halfway through cooking on each side, to end up with crisscross markings. When cooked, remove from the pan and cut roughly into chunks. Set aside.

Cut the red onions into wedges, keeping the root ends intact to hold the wedges together. Arrange in the pan and grill for 5 minutes on each side until softened and starting to brown. Remove from the pan and set aside. Place the flat pieces of red pepper in the pan, skin side down, and grill for 8 minutes on the skin side only, so that the skins are charred. Remove, set aside, then grill the asparagus in the pan for 6 minutes, turning often.

Put the boiled potatoes in a large bowl. Tear the basil, keeping a few leaves intact to garnish. Add the torn leaves to the bowl, with the chicken, onions, red pepper and asparagus. Add the olive oil and balsamic vinegar, and season. Toss the salad, season and garnish with the reserved basil and serve.

For summer chicken wraps, omit the potatoes and make the recipe as above. Warm 4 soft flour tortillas, then spread with 200 g (7 oz) hummus. Toss the griddled chicken, cut into strips, and the pan-grilled vegetables with 2 tablespoons olive oil, 2 tablespoons balsamic vinegar and a few basil leaves. Divide among the tortillas, then roll up tightly and serve, cut in half crossways, while the chicken is still warm.

fragrant tofu & noodle soup

Serves **2**

Preparation time **15 minutes**, plus draining

Cooking time **10 minutes**

125 g (4 oz) **firm tofu**, diced

1 tablespoon **sesame oil**

75 g (3 oz) **fine dried rice noodles**

600 ml (1 pint) **vegetable stock**

2.5 cm (1 inch) piece of **fresh root ginger**, peeled and thickly sliced

1 large **garlic clove**, thickly sliced

3 **kaffir lime leaves**, torn in half

2 **lemon grass stalks**, tough outer layers removed, halved

handful of **spinach** or **pak choi leaves**

50 g (2 oz) **bean sprouts**

1–2 **fresh red chillies**, deseeded and thinly sliced

2 tablespoons roughly chopped **fresh coriander**

1 tablespoon **Thai fish sauce**

Put the tofu on a plate covered with kitchen paper. Leave to stand for 10 minutes to drain.

Heat the sesame oil in a wok or large nonstick frying pan until hot, add the tofu and stir-fry for 2–3 minutes until golden brown. Remove with a slotted spoon and drain on kitchen paper.

Meanwhile, soak the rice noodles in a saucepan of boiling water for 2 minutes, then drain well.

Pour the stock into a large heavy-based saucepan. Add the ginger, garlic, lime leaves and lemon grass and bring to the boil. Reduce the heat, add the tofu, drained noodles, spinach or pak choi, bean sprouts and chillies and heat through for 2 minutes.

Stir in the coriander and fish sauce, then pour into warm deep soup bowls. Serve hot with lime wedges and chilli sauce if liked.

For Thai prawn & noodle soup, omit the tofu and soak and drain the noodles as above. Pour the vegetable stock into a saucepan and add the ginger, garlic and 2 teaspoons Thai green curry paste. Bring to the boil. Add 125 g (4 oz) thawed small frozen prawns and the drained noodles, spinach or pak choi, bean sprouts and chillies. Cook until the prawns are piping hot, then mix in the chopped coriander and serve.

beef, pumpkin & ginger stew

Serves **6**
Preparation time **20 minutes**
Cooking time **1½ hours**

2 tablespoons **plain flour**
750 g (1½ lb) **lean stewing
  beef**, diced
25 g (1 oz) **butter**
3 tablespoons **vegetable oil**
1 **onion**, chopped
2 **carrots**, sliced
2 **parsnips**, sliced
3 **bay leaves**
several **thyme sprigs**
2 tablespoons **tomato purée**
625 g (1¼ lb) **pumpkin**,
  peeled, deseeded and cut
  into small chunks
1 tablespoon **dark
  muscovado sugar**
50 g (2 oz) **fresh root ginger**,
  peeled and finely chopped
small handful of **flat leaf
  parsley**, chopped, plus extra
  to garnish
salt and **pepper**

Season the flour with salt and pepper and use to coat the beef. Melt the butter with the oil in a large saucepan over a medium-high heat. When the butter is foaming, fry the meat in 2 batches until browned all over, draining with a slotted spoon. Set aside on a plate.

Reduce the heat, add the onion, carrots and parsnips to the saucepan and fry gently for 5 minutes until softened but not coloured.

Return the meat to the pan and add the bay leaves, thyme and tomato purée. Pour in just enough water to cover the ingredients and bring slowly to the boil. Reduce the heat to its lowest setting, cover and simmer very gently for 45 minutes.

Add the pumpkin, sugar, ginger and parsley and simmer gently for a further 30 minutes until the pumpkin is soft and the meat is tender. Check the seasoning, adding salt and pepper if needed, and serve scattered with extra parsley.

For beef, sweet potato & horseradish stew, cook the recipe as above, replacing the pumpkin with 500 g (1 lb) sweet potatoes, cut into chunks, and the ginger with 3 tablespoons hot horseradish sauce.

mackerel & wild rice niçoise

Serves **3–4**
Preparation time **20 minutes**,
  plus cooling
Cooking time **25 minutes**

100 g (3½ oz) **wild rice**
150 g (5 oz) **French beans**,
  topped and tailed,
  then halved
300 g (10 oz) large **mackerel
  fillets**, pin-boned
90 ml (3½ fl oz) **olive oil**
12 **black olives**
8 **canned anchovy fillets**,
  drained and halved
250 g (8 oz) **cherry tomatoes**,
  halved
3 **hard-boiled eggs**, cut into
  quarters
1 tablespoon **lemon juice**
1 tablespoon **French mustard**
2 tablespoons chopped
  chives
salt and **pepper**

Cook the rice in plenty of boiling water for 20–25 minutes until tender. (The grains will start to split open when they are just cooked.) Add the French beans and cook for another 2 minutes.

Lay the mackerel, skin side up, on a foil-lined grill rack, while the rice is cooking. Brush with 1 tablespoon of the oil and cook under a preheated medium-hot grill for 8–10 minutes, turning after the first 5 minutes, until cooked through; the second side should not take as long to cook as the first. Leave to cool.

Drain the rice and beans and mix together in a salad bowl with the olives, anchovies, tomatoes and eggs. Flake the mackerel, discarding any stray bones, and add to the bowl.

Whisk the remaining oil with the lemon juice, mustard and chives in a small bowl, and season with a little salt and pepper. Add to the bowl.

Toss the ingredients together lightly, cover and chill until ready to serve.

For fresh tuna & wild rice niçoise, replace the mackerel with 4 x 200 g (7 oz) fresh tuna steaks, frying them in a little olive oil for 2–3 minutes on each side so that they are just pink in the centre. Continue the recipe as above.

grilled vegetable & haloumi salad

Serves **4**
Preparation time **15 minutes**
Cooking time **25 minutes**

12 **cherry tomatoes on the vine**
4 **portobello mushrooms**
olive oil
2 **courgettes**, cut into batons about 4 x 2 cm (1½ x ¾ inches)
500 g (1 lb) **fresh asparagus**, trimmed
250 g (8 oz) **haloumi cheese**, cut into 5 mm (¼ inch) slices
salt and **pepper**

Dressing
2 tablespoons **olive oil**
2 tablespoons **balsamic vinegar**

Put the tomatoes and mushrooms in a roasting tin, drizzle with about 2 tablespoons oil, season with salt and pepper, and cook in a preheated oven, 180°C (350°F), Gas Mark 4, for 10 minutes.

Put the courgettes and asparagus in a large bowl, meanwhile. Drizzle with olive oil and a pinch of salt and pepper. Heat a griddle pan over a high heat, and grill the asparagus and courgettes until starting to colour. Transfer the asparagus and courgettes to the oven with the tomatoes and mushrooms and cook for 6–8 minutes.

Use a piece of kitchen paper to wipe the griddle pan clean. Pat the cheese slices dry with kitchen paper. Heat 1 teaspoon olive oil in the pan over a medium heat. Grill the haloumi, turning once (use a fish slice or spatula to loosen the cheese first), for about 4 minutes until lightly golden with grill marks on both sides. Make the dressing by whisking together the oil and vinegar. Stack the grilled vegetables and mushrooms on 4 warm plates, dividing the ingredients evenly. Top with slices of cheese, spoon over the dressing and serve immediately.

For watermelon & haloumi cheese, cut 250 g (8 oz) haloumi cheese into thin slices. Heat 1 tablespoon olive oil in a large nonstick frying pan over a medium heat and cook the cheese for about 4 minutes until golden and crispy on both sides. Drain and pat dry with kitchen paper. Halve, peel and deseed ½ small watermelon and cut the flesh into small triangles. Toss the melon with a small bunch of chopped mint and the diced flesh of 1 ripe halved, stoned and peeled avocado. Serve with the grilled haloumi.

turkey & orange stir-fry

Serves **4**
Preparation time **30 minutes**,
   plus marinating
Cooking time **10 minutes**

375 g (12 oz) **boneless,
   skinless turkey breast**, cut
   into large chunks or strips
grated rind and juice of
   2 **oranges**
1 tablespoon **cornflour**
1 tablespoon **vegetable oil**
½ **red pepper**, cored,
   deseeded and cut into strips
½ **green pepper**, cored,
   deseeded and cut into strips
3 **celery sticks**, cut into cubes
125 g (4 oz) **carrots**, cut into
   thin slices
salt and **pepper**

Marinade
1 tablespoon **light soy sauce**
2 tablespoons **orange juice**

Make the marinade first. Mix together the soy sauce
and orange juice in a bowl or shallow dish. Add the
turkey to the marinade, cover with clingfilm and leave
to marinate in the refrigerator for 30 minutes.

Mix the orange juice with enough water to make
150 ml (¼ pint). Add the cornflour and season with
a dash of salt and pepper. Stir until the cornflour has
dissolved, then set aside.

Remove the turkey from the marinade with a slotted
spoon, and put on a plate. Keep the marinade.

Heat the oil in a wok or large frying pan over a medium-
high heat. Add the turkey and stir-fry for 4–5 minutes,
then add the orange rind, red and green peppers, celery
and carrots. Stir-fry for another 3 minutes.

Stir the cornflour mixture, then add it and the reserved
marinade to the wok or frying pan. Bring to the boil,
and stir well for a minute or so until the sauce starts to
thicken and becomes glossy. Serve immediately on a
mound of boiled rice.

For turkey & mixed vegetable stir-fry, marinate the
turkey and make up the orange sauce as above. Stir-fry
the turkey until just cooked through, then add a 275 g
(9 oz) packet of ready-prepared stir-fried vegetables
and 2 chopped garlic cloves. Stir-fry for 2–3 minutes,
pour in the orange sauce and marinade and cook until
the sauce has thickened.

kale soup with garlic croutons

Serves **8**
Preparation time **25 minutes**
Cooking time **45 minutes**

50 g (2 oz) **butter**
1 **onion**, chopped
2 **carrots**, sliced
500 g (1 lb) **kale**, tough
  stalks discarded
1.2 litres (2 pints) **water**
600 ml (1 pint) **vegetable
  stock**
1 tablespoon **lemon juice**
300 g (10 oz) **potatoes**, sliced
pinch of grated **nutmeg**
salt and **pepper**
2 **kale leaves**, thinly shredded,
  to garnish

Garlic croutons
90–125 ml (3½–4 fl oz) **olive
  oil**
3 **garlic cloves**, sliced
6–8 slices **wholemeal bread,**
  crusts removed, cut into
  1 cm (½ inch) cubes

Melt the butter in a large saucepan, add the onion and cook over a medium heat for 5 minutes or until soft. Add the carrots and kale in batches, stirring constantly. Cook for 2 minutes until the kale has just wilted.

Pour in the measurement water and stock, then add the lemon juice, potatoes and nutmeg. Season with salt and pepper. Bring to the boil, then reduce the heat, cover and simmer for 30–35 minutes until all the vegetables are tender. Add a little water if the soup is too thick.

Make the croutons while the soup is cooking. Heat the oil in a large frying pan, add the garlic and cook over a medium heat for 1 minute. Add the bread cubes and cook, turning frequently, until golden brown. Remove with a slotted spoon and drain on kitchen paper. Remove and discard the garlic. Add the shredded kale to the pan and cook, stirring constantly, until crispy.

Reheat the soup gently. Serve in warm soup bowls, garnished with the croutons and crispy shredded kale.

For caldo verde, heat 2 tablespoons olive oil in a pan. Add 2 chopped onions, 100 g (3½ oz) diced chorizo sausage and fry over a medium heat until golden. Add the carrots and kale as above, mixing in 2 chopped garlic cloves and 1 teaspoon smoked paprika, taking care that the paprika does not burn and turn bitter. Continue the recipe as above.

beetroot, spinach & orange salad

Serves **4**

Preparation time **20 minutes**, plus cooling

Cooking time **1–2 hours**

500 g (1 lb) **uncooked beetroot,** preferably of a similar size

2 **garlic cloves**, peeled but left whole

handful of **oregano leaves**

1 teaspoon **vegetable oil**

1 tablespoon **balsamic vinegar**

200 g (7 oz) **baby spinach**

2 **oranges**, peeled, any white pith removed and cut into segments

salt and **pepper**

Vinaigrette

1 tablespoon **balsamic vinegar**

1 teaspoon **Dijon mustard**

4 tablespoons **olive oil**

pinch of **sugar** (optional)

Put the whole beetroots in the centre of a large piece of foil, along with the garlic and oregano. Sprinkle with pepper and drizzle over the vegetable oil and vinegar. Gather up the foil loosely and fold over at the top to seal it. Place on a baking sheet and bake in a preheated oven, 200°C (400°F), Gas Mark 6, for 1–2 hours (depending on how large the beetroot are) until tender.

Unwrap the foil parcel and leave the beetroot to cool before peeling and slicing them. Discard the garlic. Make the vinaigrette. Mix together the balsamic vinegar and mustard in a small bowl. Season with a little salt and pepper. Gradually add the olive oil, whisking constantly, until smooth and well combined. Taste and adjust the seasoning as needed, adding a pinch of sugar to reduce the acidity, if liked, bearing in mind the sweetness of the roasted beetroot. Whisk again until the sugar has dissolved. Alternatively, put all the vinaigrette ingredients in a screw-top jar, seal tightly and shake vigorously until well combined.

Put the spinach in a large bowl, and gently toss together with beetroot and orange. Drizzle over the vinaigrette, sprinkle with pepper and tuck in.

For beetroot, spinach & goats' cheese salad,

prepare and roast the beetroot as above. Cool, peel and slice, then put in a salad bowl with the spinach and vinaigrette dressing. Lightly toast 4 slices ciabatta or French bread on both sides under a preheated grill. Cut a 100 g (3½ oz) goats' cheese into 4 slices and arrange on top of the toasted bread. Cook under the hot grill for a few minutes until the cheese has melted, then serve on a bed of salad.

griddled chicken fajitas

Serves **4**

Preparation time **20 minutes**,
plus marinating

Cooking time **16–20 minutes**

4 **boneless, skinless chicken
breasts**, about 125 g
(4 oz) each

4 ripe **tomatoes**

4 large **soft flour tortillas**

150 ml (¼ pint) **soured cream**

1 **avocado**, halved, stoned,
peeled and sliced

4 **spring onions**, sliced

½ **red onion**, finely chopped

tortilla chips, to serve
(optional)

salt and **pepper**

Marinade

2 tablespoons **light soy sauce**

3 cm (1¼ inch) piece of **fresh
root ginger**, peeled and
finely chopped

2 **garlic cloves**, finely chopped

2 tablespoons **olive oil**

1 bunch of **fresh coriander**,
chopped

1 **fresh red chilli**, deseeded
and chopped

2 tablespoons **lime juice**

Combine all the ingredients for the marinade in a
shallow dish. Add the chicken breasts, and leave to
marinate at room temperature for 2 hours, or in the
refrigerator for 24 hours. Put the tomatoes in a bowl, and
pour over boiling water to cover. Leave for 1–2 minutes,
then drain, cut a cross at the stem end of each tomato
and peel off the skins. Cut the tomatoes into slices.

Heat a griddle pan or ordinary frying pan. Place the
marinated chicken breasts in the pan and cook for
8–10 minutes on each side. If you are using a griddle
pan, cook the chicken on each side without moving it
in the pan, so that it ends up with a distinct striped
pattern of grill marks; if you like, change the position of
the chicken halfway through cooking on each side, to
end up with crisscross markings. When cooked, remove
the chicken from the pan and slice into long strips.

Place the tortillas under a preheated grill and cook for
30 seconds on each side until warmed through but not
crisp. Spread a spoonful of soured cream over one side
of each tortilla, then add a little tomato, avocado and a
sprinkling of spring onions and red onion. Arrange the
pieces of griddled chicken on top and season with salt
and pepper. Roll up each tortilla tightly and cut in half
crossways. Serve with tortilla chips, if liked.

For guacamole, to accompany the fajitas, halve and
stone 2 ripe avocados. Scoop out the flesh, put in a
bowl and mash with a fork. Mix with the juice of 1 lime,
3 tablespoons chopped fresh coriander, 1 skinned and
finely diced tomato and, if liked, 1 finely chopped jalapeño
chilli. Spoon onto the tortillas instead of soured cream.

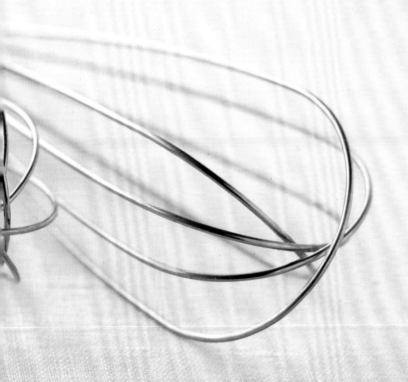

sweet treats

easy chocolate fudge cake

Cuts into **12**
Preparation time **10 minutes**,
   plus cooling and setting time
Cooking time **50–55 minutes**

250 g (8 oz) **plain dark**
   chocolate, broken
   into pieces
200 g (7 oz) **butter**
4 **eggs**, beaten
125 g (4 oz) **caster sugar**
225 g (7½ oz) **self-raising**
   flour, sifted

Icing
175 g (6 oz) **plain dark**
   chocolate, broken into
   pieces
150 ml (¼ pint) **single cream**

Grease a 20 x 30 cm (8 x 12 inch) baking tin lightly and line with nonstick baking paper, snipping diagonally into the corners of the paper and pressing it into the tin to line the base and sides. Put the chocolate and butter in a heatproof bowl set over a saucepan of gently simmering water (don't let the bowl touch the water) and stir over a low heat until melted. Leave to cool for 5 minutes.

Whisk together the eggs and sugar in a bowl for 5 minutes until thick, while the cake is cooking. Beat in the cooled chocolate mixture and fold in the flour.

Spoon the mixture into the prepared tin and bake in a preheated oven, 160°C (325°F), Gas Mark 3, for 45–50 minutes until risen and firm to the touch. Leave to cool in the tin for 10 minutes, then turn out on to a wire rack to cool completely, removing the paper from the base.

Make the icing, meanwhile. Put the chocolate in a saucepan with the cream and heat gently, stirring, until melted. Leave to cool for 1 hour until thickened to a pouring consistency, then spread over the cake. Leave to set for 30 minutes before serving.

For fudge cake with chocolate butter icing, instead of the ganache icing above, put 200 g (7 oz) unsalted butter, at room temperature, in a bowl. Gradually beat in 200 g (7 oz) sifted icing sugar and 50 g (2 oz) sifted cocoa powder until smooth. Spread over the cooled cake and decorate with 50 g (2 oz) grated milk chocolate.

warm summer fruit trifle

Makes **6**
Preparation time **20 minutes**
Cooking time **20 minutes**

8 **sponge fingers** or 100 g
    (3½ oz) **plain sponge** or
    jam-filled Swiss roll
3 tablespoons **orange juice**
375 g (12 oz) **frozen mixed
    summer fruits**, just thawed
425 g (14 oz) **ready-made
    custard**

Meringue topping
3 **egg whites**
75 g (3 oz) **granulated sugar**

Crumble the sponge fingers or cake into the bottom of 6 individual ovenproof dishes. Drizzle the orange juice over the tops, then add the mixed fruits. Dollop the custard over the tops.

Whisk the egg whites in a clean, dry bowl until stiff peaks form, then gradually whisk in the sugar, a spoonful at a time, until all the sugar has been added. Keep whisking for another 1–2 minutes until the mixture is thick and glossy.

Spoon the meringue mixture over the top of the custard in large swirls. Place the dishes on a baking sheet. Cook in a preheated oven, 160°C (325°F), Gas Mark 3, for 20 minutes until the meringue is golden brown on top. Serve warm.

For chilled summer fruit trifle, in the bottom of a large bowl, sprinkle the crumbled sponge finger biscuits or cake with 3 tablespoons sherry. Top with the thawed fruits, then the custard. Whip 150 ml (¼ pint) double cream until it forms soft swirls. Spoon over the top of the trifle instead of the meringue. Chill until ready to serve, then decorate with sugar sprinkles or 4 teaspoons toasted flaked almonds.

lemon sorbet

Serves **4**

Preparation time **15 minutes**, plus chilling and freezing

125 g (4 oz) **caster sugar**

5 tablespoons **boiling water**

500 ml (17 fl oz) freshly squeezed **lemon juice** (about 10 lemons)

lemon rind curls, to decorate (use a zester to make the curls)

shortbread biscuits, to serve

Put the sugar in a heatproof jug. Pour over the measurement water and stir until the sugar has started to dissolve. Pour in the lemon juice and stir well until all the sugar has dissolved.

Pour the mixture into a shallow freezerproof container and cover with clingfilm. Chill for 30 minutes.

Churn in an ice-cream machine according to the manufacturer's instructions. Alternatively, freeze in the same container, beating the sorbet with a whisk at 45-minute intervals to break up the ice crystals, until almost completely frozen. Process the sorbet in a food processor or blender until smooth. Freeze until solid.

Transfer to the refrigerator 10 minutes before serving to soften slightly. Serve in individual bowls or glasses, decorated with lemon rind curls and accompanied by shortbread biscuits. The sorbet is best eaten on the day it is made.

For gin & lemon float, make up the sorbet as above, stirring in 6 tablespoons gin. Freeze as above. Pour 1 litre (1¾ pint) fizzy lemonade into glasses, top with scoops of the sorbet and decorate with slices of lime. Serve immediately with spoons and straws.

jam roly-poly

Serves **6**
Preparation time **25 minutes**
Cooking time **2 hours**

300 g (10 oz) **self-raising flour**
1 teaspoon **baking powder**
150 g (5 oz) **shredded vegetable suet**
75 g (3 oz) **caster sugar**
50 g (2 oz) **fresh breadcrumbs**
finely grated rind of 1 **lemon**
finely grated rind of 1 **orange**
1 **egg**, beaten
175–200 ml (6–7 fl oz) **milk**
6 tablespoons **raspberry jam**
150 g (5 oz) **frozen raspberries**, just thawed

Put the flour, baking powder, suet and sugar in a bowl, then stir in the breadcrumbs and lemon and orange rinds. Add the egg, then gradually mix in enough of the milk to make a soft but not sticky dough.

Knead the dough lightly, then roll out to a 30 cm (12 inch) square. Spread with the jam, leaving a 2.5 cm (1 inch) border round the edges, then sprinkle the raspberries on top. Brush the border with a little milk, then roll up the pastry. Wrap loosely in nonstick baking paper, twisting the edges together and leaving space for the pudding to rise, then wrap loosely in foil.

Put on a roasting rack set over a large roasting tin, then carefully pour boiling water into the tin but not over the roasting rack (the water must not touch the wrapped pudding). Cover the tin with foil and twist over the edges to seal well. Bake in a preheated oven, 150°C (300°F), Gas Mark 2, for 2 hours until the pudding is well risen. Check once or twice during baking and top up the water level if needed. Transfer the pudding to a chopping board using a clean tea towel. Unwrap and discard the baking paper, cut the roly-poly into thick slices and serve with hot custard.

For spotted dick, warm 3 tablespoons orange juice or rum in a small saucepan. Add 150 g (5 oz) raisins, 1 teaspoon ground ginger and ¼ teaspoon grated nutmeg and leave to soak for 1 hour or longer. Add to the flour mixture just before adding the egg and milk. Shape the dough into a long sausage, wrap in nonstick baking paper and foil and steam in the oven as above. Serve in thick slices with hot custard flavoured with a little extra rum, if liked.

rum & raisin chocolate brownies

Cuts into **20**
Preparation time **30 minutes**,
  plus soaking
Cooking time **25–30 minutes**

3 tablespoons **white** or **dark
  rum**
100 g (3½ oz) **raisins**
250 g (8 oz) **plain dark
  chocolate**, broken into
  pieces
250 g (8 oz) **butter**
4 **eggs**
200 g (7 oz) **caster sugar**
75 g (3 oz) **self-raising flour**
1 teaspoon **baking powder**
100 g (3½ oz) **white** or **milk
  chocolate**

Warm the rum gently in a small saucepan. Add the
raisins and leave to soak for 2 hours or overnight.
Heat the dark chocolate and butter gently in a saucepan
until both have just melted, taking care not to scorch
the chocolate.

Whisk together the eggs and sugar in a bowl using
an electric mixer until the mixture is very thick and the
whisk leaves a trail when lifted above it.

Fold the warm chocolate and butter into the whisked
eggs and sugar. Sift the flour and baking powder over
the top, then fold through. Pour the mixture into a lightly
greased 18 x 28 cm (7 x 11 inch) roasting tin lined
with nonstick baking paper and ease into the corners.
Spoon the rum-soaked raisins over the top. Bake in
a preheated oven, 180°C (350°F), Gas Mark 4, for
25–30 minutes until well risen; the top should be crusty
and cracked and the centre still slightly soft. Leave to
cool and harden in the tin.

Lift out of the tin using the lining paper. To make the
topping, melt the white or milk chocolate in a heatproof
bowl set over a saucepan of gently simmering water
(don't let the bowl touch the water), then drizzle over
the top of the brownies. Leave to harden, then cut into
20 even-sized pieces. Peel off and discard the paper.
Store the brownies in an airtight tin for up to 3 days.

For triple chocolate brownies, omit the rum-soaked
raisins and instead sprinkle 100 g (3½ oz) finely
chopped milk chocolate and 100 g (3½ oz) finely
chopped white chocolate over the mixture just before
baking. Bake as above, then omit the chocolate topping.

almond angel cakes with berries

Serves **6**
Preparation time **15 minutes**
Cooking time **10–12 minutes**

4 **egg whites**
3 tablespoons **granulated
  sugar**
50 g (2 oz) **ground almonds**
generous pinch of **cream
  of tartar**
15 g (½ oz) **flaked almonds**
1 tablespoon sifted **icing
  sugar**, to dust (optional)

Berries with fromage frais
200 g (7 oz) **fromage frais**
2 tablespoons **clear honey** or
  sifted icing sugar (optional)
400 g (13 oz) **frozen mixed
  berry fruits**, just thawed

Brush 6 holes of a deep muffin tin with a little sunflower oil and line the bases with rounds of greaseproof paper. Whisk the egg whites in a clean, dry bowl until stiff, moist peaks form. Whisk in the granulated sugar, a teaspoonful at a time, until it has all been added. Keep whisking for 1–2 minutes until thick and glossy.

Fold in the ground almonds and cream of tartar, then spoon the mixture into the prepared sections of the muffin tin. Sprinkle the flaked almonds over the top of each one. Bake in a preheated oven, 180°C (350°F), Gas Mark 4, for 10–12 minutes until golden brown and set. Carefully loosen the edges of the cakes with a knife, then lift on to a wire rack to cool.

Put the fromage frais in a bowl and stir through the honey or icing sugar to sweeten, if liked. Swirl the thawed berry fruits through the fromage frais. Arrange the angel cakes on a serving plate, dusted with the icing sugar, if liked. Serve with the swirled fruits and fromage frais for spooning over.

For almond meringues, whisk the 4 egg whites until stiff peaks form, then gradually whisk in 225 g (7½ oz) caster sugar until all the sugar has dissolved and the mixture is thick and glossy. Fold in 50 g (2 oz) finely chopped toasted flaked almonds. Scoop dessertspoons of the mixture on to a baking sheet lined with nonstick baking paper. Cook in a preheated oven, 110°C (225°F), Gas mark ½, for 1 hour or until the meringues lift easily off the paper. Leave to cool in the oven with the door ajar, then remove and cool completely. Sandwich together with 200 ml (7 fl oz) whipped double cream.

lemon meringue pie

Serves **6**
Preparation time **40 minutes**,
   plus chilling and standing
Cooking time **35–40 minutes**

375 g (12 oz) chilled **ready-
   made** or **homemade sweet
   shortcrust pastry**
200 g (7 oz) **caster sugar**
40 g (1 ½ oz) **cornflour**
grated rind and juice of
   2 **lemons**
4 **eggs**, separated
200–250 ml (7–8 fl oz) **water**

Roll out the pastry thinly on a lightly floured surface and use to line a 20 cm (8 inch) diameter x 5 cm (2 inch) deep loose-bottomed fluted flan tin, pressing into the sides. Trim the top and prick the bottom of the pastry case with a fork. Chill for 15 minutes, then line with nonstick baking paper, add macaroni or beans and bake in a preheated oven, 190°C (375°F), Gas Mark 5, for 15 minutes. Remove the paper and macaroni or beans and bake for a further 5 minutes until crisp and golden.

Put 75 g (3 oz) of the sugar in a bowl with the cornflour and lemon rind. Add the egg yolks and mix until smooth. Make the lemon juice up to 300 ml (½ pint) with water, pour into a saucepan and bring to the boil. Gradually mix into the yolk mixture, whisking until smooth. Pour back in the pan and bring to the boil, whisking until very thick. Pour into the pastry case and spread level. Set aside.

Whisk the egg whites in a clean, dry bowl until they form stiff peaks. Gradually whisk in the remaining sugar, a teaspoonful at a time, then keep whisking for 1–2 minutes more until thick and glossy. Spoon the meringue mixture over the lemon layer to cover completely and swirl with a spoon. Reduce the oven temperature to 180°C (350°F), Gas Mark 4, and cook the pie for 15–20 minutes until the meringue is golden and cooked through. Leave for 15 minutes, then carefully remove the tart tin and transfer to a serving plate. Serve warm or cold with cream.

For citrus meringue pie, mix the grated rind of 1 lime, 1 lemon and ½ small orange with the cornflour. Squeeze the juice from the fruits and make up to 300 ml (½ pint) with water. Continue the recipe as above.

peanut butter cookies

Makes **32**

Preparation time **10 minutes**

Cooking time **12 minutes**

125 g (4 oz) **unsalted butter,**
   at room temperature

150 g (5 oz) **soft brown sugar**

125 g (4 oz) **crunchy peanut
   butter**

1 **egg**, lightly beaten

150 g (5 oz) **plain flour**

½ teaspoon **baking powder**

125 g (4 oz) **unsalted
   peanuts**

Beat together the butter and sugar in a bowl or food
processor until pale and creamy. Add the peanut butter,
egg, flour and baking powder and stir together until
combined. Stir in the peanuts.

Drop large teaspoonfuls of the mixture on to 3 large,
lightly oiled baking sheets, leaving 5 cm (2 inch) gaps
between each one for them to spread during cooking.

Flatten the mounds slightly with a fork and bake in
a preheated oven, 190°C (375°F), Gas Mark 5, for
12 minutes until golden around the edges. Leave to
cool on the baking sheets for 2 minutes, then transfer
to a wire rack to cool completely.

For peanut butter & chocolate chip cookies, use
only 50 g (2 oz) unsalted peanuts and add 100 g
(3½ oz) milk chocolate chips. Make and bake the
cookies as above.

banoffee pie

Serves **6**
Preparation time **35 minutes**,
  plus chilling and cooling
Cooking time **8 minutes**

200 g (7 oz) **unsalted butter**
2 tablespoons **golden syrup**
250 g (8 oz) **digestive
  biscuits**, crushed
100 g (3½ oz) **dark
  muscovado sugar**
400 g (13 oz) can **full-fat
  condensed milk**
300 ml (½ pint) **double cream**
3 small ripe **bananas**
juice of **1 lemon**
plain dark chocolate, grated,
  to decorate

Melt half the butter and the syrup in a saucepan, add
the biscuit crumbs and mix well. Tip into a greased
20 cm (8 inch) springform tin and press evenly over
the base and up the sides almost to the tin's top. Chill.

Heat the remaining butter and the sugar in a nonstick
frying pan until the butter has melted and the sugar
dissolved. Add the condensed milk and cook over a
medium heat, stirring continuously, for 4–5 minutes
until the mixture thickens and begins to smell of caramel
(do not have the heat too high or the condensed milk
will burn).

Remove the pan from the heat and leave the mixture
to cool for 1–2 minutes, then pour into the biscuit case.
Allow to cool completely, then chill for at least 1 hour.

Whip the cream, just before serving, until soft peaks
form. Peel and halve the bananas lengthways, then cut
into slices and toss in the lemon juice. Fold two-thirds
of the banana slices into the cream, then spoon over
the toffee layer. Arrange the remaining bananas on
top. Loosen the edge of the biscuit crust with a palette
knife, then remove the tin and transfer the pie to a
serving plate. Sprinkle with grated chocolate and serve
cut into slices.

For banoffee ice cream sundae, omit the biscuit
base and make the toffee sauce as above, but cook for
just 2 minutes so that it is runnier. Leave to cool. Layer
the sliced bananas evenly in 6 serving glasses with
12 scoops vanilla ice cream, 6 crumbled brandy snap
biscuits and a drizzle of the sauce, reheated if very thick.
Sprinkle with chocolate curls or grated chocolate.

chunky monkeys

Makes **12**
Preparation time **10 minutes**
Cooking time **10–12 minutes**

200 g (7 oz) **plain flour**
1 teaspoon **bicarbonate**
  of soda
125 g (4 oz) **sugar**
125 g (4 oz) **butter**, cut
  into cubes
1 **egg**
1 tablespoon **milk**
150 g (5 oz) **white chocolate**,
  roughly chopped
75 g (3 oz) **glacé cherries**,
  roughly chopped

Put the flour, bicarbonate of soda and sugar in a bowl and mix through. Add the butter and rub in with the fingertips until the mixture resembles breadcrumbs.

Beat together the egg and milk in a separate bowl. Add the chopped chocolate and glacé cherries, then mix into the flour mixture and stir well until smooth.

Drop heaped spoonfuls of the cookie mixture, well spaced apart, on to a greased baking sheet and bake in a preheated oven, 180°C (350°F), Gas Mark 4, for 10–12 minutes until lightly golden. Leave to harden on the tray for 2 minutes, then slide off on to a wire rack or plate to cool.

For double chocolate chunky monkeys, replace 15 g (½ oz) of the flour with 15 g (½ oz) cocoa powder. Continue the recipe as above, adding the roughly chopped white chocolate and 75 g (3 oz) toasted blanched hazelnuts, roughly chopped, instead of the cherries. Bake as above.

really easy fruit cake

Serves **8**
Preparation time **20 minutes**
Cooking time **1–1¼ hours**

250 g (8 oz) **self-raising flour**
½ teaspoon **ground mixed spice**
½ teaspoon **ground cinnamon**
125 g (4 oz) **butter** or **margarine**
125 g (4 oz) **soft brown sugar**
125 g (4 oz) **currants**
50 g (2 oz) **glacé cherries**, quartered
1 large **egg**
75 ml (3 fl oz) **milk**
demerara sugar, for sprinkling (optional)

Mix together the flour, mixed spice and cinnamon in a large bowl. Add the butter and rub in with your fingertips until the mixture resembles breadcrumbs. Stir in the sugar, currants and glacé cherries.

Whisk together the egg and milk in a separate bowl, add to the fruit mixture and beat thoroughly.

Pour the mixture into a greased 20 cm (8 inch) square cake tin lined with nonstick baking paper. Sprinkle the top with a little demerara sugar, if liked. Bake in a preheated oven, 180°C (350°F), Gas Mark 4, for 1–1¼ hours until the top is firm but springy to the touch; a skewer inserted into the centre of the cake should come out clean. Leave to stand in the tin for a few minutes, then turn out on to a wire rack to cool completely. Cut into squares to serve.

For fruited date & orange cake, make up the spiced crumb mixture as above, then stir in the grated rind of 1 orange and 175 g (6 oz) chopped ready-to-eat dates. Stir in the egg and milk mixture, spoon into the prepared tin and cook as above.

raspberry mallow fondue

Serves **4**
Preparation time **5 minutes**
Cooking time **10 minutes**

250 g (8 oz) **raspberries**
175 g (6 oz) **marshmallows**
175 ml (6 fl oz) **double cream**
few drops of **lemon juice**

To serve
raspberries, **marshmallows**
   and **shortbread biscuits**,
      for dipping

Purée the raspberries in a blender or food processor until smooth, or rub through a sieve into a bowl.

Put the puréed raspberries, marshmallows and cream in the fondue pot and melt over a low heat, stirring constantly. Add the lemon juice and heat through, but do not allow to boil.

Move the fondue pot to the table and keep warm on a burner, then gather all your friends round and dip the biscuits, raspberries and marshmallows into the raspberry mallow, while still warm.

For peach mallow fondue, make a cross cut in 1 large ripe peach, put in a bowl, cover with boiling water and leave for 1 minute. Drain and peel off the skin. Cut the peach in half, remove and discard the stone and roughly chop the flesh. Purée in a blender or food processor until smooth, or rub through a sieve. Heat with the marshmallows and cream as above. Serve with peach slices and biscuits as above.

chocolate overload

Serves **4**
Preparation time **8 minutes**

8 **chocolate cream sandwich
    biscuits**, crushed
25 g (1 oz) **butter**, melted
500 ml (17 fl oz) tub
    **chocolate cookie dough ice
    cream**, softened
2 tablespoons **runny caramel
    sauce** or **dulce de leche**
    (optional)

To decorate
white chocolate shavings
milk chocolate shavings

Mix the crushed biscuits with the melted butter, then press firmly into the bottom of 4 dessert dishes.

Scoop the ice cream over the top of the biscuit bases. Drizzle with the caramel or spoon over the dulce de leche, if using, and decorate with white and milk chocolate shavings. Serve immediately.

For chocolate sundaes with raspberries, replace the crushed biscuits with 20 mini meringues and omit the butter. Layer the ice cream, meringues and 200 g (7 oz) raspberries in serving glasses. Drizzle with single cream and top with grated chocolate.

fruit fritters

Serves **2**
Preparation time **15 minutes**
Cooking time **10 minutes**

40 g (1 ½ oz) **plain flour**
pinch of **ground mixed spice**
pinch of **salt**
1 **egg**, separated
15 g (½ oz) **butter**, melted
75 ml (3 fl oz) **sparkling water**
vegetable oil, for deep-frying
1 firm, ripe **banana**
1 firm, ripe **peach** or **nectarine**
1 crisp **dessert apple**
icing sugar, to dust

Mix the flour with a pinch of mixed spice and salt in a bowl. Beat in the egg yolk, melted butter and sparkling water to make a smooth batter.

Whisk the egg white in a clean, dry bowl until stiff peaks form, then gently fold into the batter.

Heat 2.5 cm (1 inch) of vegetable oil in a deep heavy-based saucepan or deep-fat fryer until hot – 180°C (350°C), or until a cube of bread dropped into the oil browns in 30 seconds.

Peel and thickly slice the banana, meanwhile, then stone and slice the peach, and core and thickly slice the apple.

Dip the slices of fruit into the batter and deep-fry for 1–2 minutes, in batches, until crisp and golden. Drain on kitchen paper.

Dust the fritters with a little icing sugar and serve piping hot with ice cream.

For apple fritters with berry sauce, thaw 200 g (7 oz) frozen mixed blackberries, raspberries and cherries, then purée in a blender or food processor with 2 tablespoons icing sugar, or rub through a sieve. Pour into a jug. Make up the fritter batter as above and use to coat 3 cored and sliced apples. Deep-fry as above. Dust with icing sugar and serve piping hot with the berry sauce.

orchard fruit crumble

Serves **6**
Preparation time **20 minutes**
Cooking time **30–35 minutes**

2 **dessert apples**
2 ripe **pears**
400 g (13 oz) **red plums**,
  quartered and pitted
2 tablespoons **water**
75 g (3 oz) **caster sugar**
100 g (3½ oz) **plain flour**
50 g (2 oz) **unsalted butter**,
  diced
50 g (2 oz) **desiccated
  coconut**
50 g (2 oz) **milk chocolate
  chips**

Peel, core and quarter the apples and pears. Slice the quarters and add the slices to a 1.2 litre (2 pint) pie dish. Add the plums and the measurement water, then sprinkle with 25 g (1 oz) of the sugar. Cover the dish with foil and bake in a preheated oven, 180°C (350°F), Gas Mark 4, for 10 minutes.

Put the remaining sugar in a bowl with the flour, add the butter and rub in with your fingertips or an electric mixer until the mixture resembles fine breadcrumbs. Stir in the coconut and chocolate chips.

Remove the foil from the fruit and spoon the crumble over the top. Bake for 20–25 minutes until the crumble topping is golden brown and the fruit is tender. Serve warm with custard or cream.

For plum & orange crumble, put 750 g (1½ lb) plums, quartered and pitted, into a 1.2 litre (2 pint) pie dish with 50 g (2 oz) caster sugar, omitting the apples and pears. Make the crumble as above, adding the grated rind of 1 small orange and 50 g (2 oz) ground almonds instead of the desiccated coconut and chocolate chips. Bake as above.

caffè latte custards

Serves **6**
Preparation time **20 minutes**, plus chilling
Cooking time **30 minutes**

2 **eggs**
2 **egg yolks**
397 g (13 oz) can **full-fat condensed milk**
200 ml (7 fl oz) **strong black coffee**
150 ml (¼ pint) **double cream**
cocoa powder to dust
chocolate wafer biscuits, to serve

Whisk together the eggs, egg yolks and condensed milk in a bowl until just combined. Gradually whisk in the coffee until blended.

Strain the mixture through a sieve, then pour into 6 small 125 ml (4 fl oz) greased coffee cups. Transfer the cups to a roasting tin. Pour enough hot water into the tin to come halfway up the sides of the cups, then cook in a preheated oven, 160°C (325°F), Gas Mark 3, for 30 minutes until just set.

Lift the cups out of the water, leave to cool on a wire rack, then transfer to the refrigerator and chill for 4–5 hours.

Whip the cream until it forms soft swirls, when ready to serve. Spoon the cream over the top of the desserts, dust with a little sifted cocoa powder and serve with the chocolate wafer biscuits.

For dark chocolate custards, bring 450 ml (¾ pint) milk and 150 ml (¼ pint) double cream just to the boil in a saucepan. Remove from the heat and add 200 g (7 oz) plain dark chocolate, broken into pieces; leave to melt. In a bowl, whisk together 2 eggs plus 2 egg yolks with 50 g (2 oz) caster sugar and ¼ teaspoon ground cinnamon until light and creamy. Gradually mix in the chocolate mixture and stir until smooth. Strain into small dishes and bake as above. Top with softly whipped cream and chocolate curls.

drinks

sea breeze

Makes **2**

Preparation time **3 minutes**

ice cubes
2 measures **vodka**
4 measures **cranberry juice**
2 measures **grapefruit juice**
lime wedges, to decorate

Fill 2 highball glasses with ice cubes, pour over the vodka, cranberry juice and grapefruit juice and stir well.

Decorate with lime wedges and serve with straws for drinking, if liked.

For bay breeze, a sweeter drink, replace the grapefruit juice with 2 measures pineapple juice, which contrasts well with the slightly bitter taste of the cranberry juice.

mojito

Makes **2**
Preparation time **3 minutes**

16 **mint leaves** (including
   stalks), plus extra sprigs
   to decorate
1 **lime**, cut into wedges
4 teaspoons **cane sugar**
crushed **ice**
5 measures **white rum**
soda water, to top up

Muddle the mint leaves, lime and sugar in the bottom of 2 highball glasses using a muddling stick or a long-handled teaspoon, gently pressing down and stirring to release the flavours. Fill the glasses with crushed ice.

Add the rum, stir and top up with soda water.

Decorate with mint sprigs and serve.

For limon mojito, a citrus version of the classic mojito, muddle 2 lime quarters with 4 teaspoons soft brown sugar and 16 mint leaves in the bottom of 2 highball glasses. Add crushed ice and replace the white rum with 4 measures Limon Bacardi. Stir and top up with soda water, if liked. Decorate with lemon and lime slices and drink through straws.

hawaiian vodka

Serves **1**
Preparation time **3 minutes**

4–5 **ice cubes**
1 teaspoon **grenadine**
1 measure **pineapple juice**
juice of 1 **lemon**
juice of 1 **orange**
3 measures **vodka**
slice of **lemon**, to decorate

Put the ice cubes in a highball glass and drizzle over the grenadine. Mix together the pineapple, lemon and orange juices and add to the glass with the vodka.

Alternatively, put the ice cubes in a cocktail shaker or screw-top jar. Pour the grenadine, fruit juices, grenadine and vodka over the ice and shake until a frost forms. Strain into a highball glass.

Decorate with a lemon slice and serve.

For a non-alcoholic Hawaiian cocktail, mix together 2 measures pineapple juice, 2 measures mango juice, the juice of 1 lemon and the juice of 1 orange in a jug. Pour 1 teaspoon grenadine over ice cubes in a tall glass, then pour over the fruit juice.

sangria

Serves **10**

Preparation time **8 minutes**,
  plus chilling

20–30 **ice cubes**

2 x 75 cl bottles **light Spanish red wine**, chilled

125 ml (4 fl oz) **brandy** (optional)

450 ml (¾ pint) **soda water**, chilled

slices of **fruit** such as **apples, pears, oranges, lemons, peaches** and **strawberries**

slices of **orange**, to decorate

Put the ice in a large serving jug, and pour over the wine and brandy, if using. Give everything a stir.

Add the soda water and the slices of fruit. Leave, covered, in the refrigerator until you wish to serve.

Decorate the side of each glass with an orange slice, pour in the sangria and serve.

For white sangria, mix 2 x 75 cl bottles Spanish white wine such as Rioja with the brandy and 6 tablespoons caster sugar. Stir until the sugar has dissolved, then add the ice, soda water, fruit and sprigs of mint.

hangover express

Serves **1**
Preparation time **5 minutes**

150 g (5 oz) **broccoli**, broken
   into florets
2 **dessert apples**, cored and
   quartered
150 g (5 oz) **spinach**
ice cubes

Juice the broccoli, apples and spinach in a juicer or blender, alternating the spinach with the broccoli and apple so that the machine does not get clogged up with the leaves.

Mix with a couple of ice cubes before serving, to dilute slightly, as this juice is very sweet.

For broccoli & express, juice the broccoli and dessert apples, then stir in 1 tablespoon fresh lemon juice. Serve with ice.

hot chocolate

Serves **4**
Preparation time **10 minutes**
Cooking time **15 minutes**

100 g (3½ oz) good-quality
  plain dark chocolate,
  broken into small pieces
25 g (1 oz) **caster sugar**
750 ml (1¼ pints) **milk**
a few drops of **vanilla extract**
pinch of **ground cinnamon**
3 tablespoons **Kahlua** or other
  coffee liqueur (optional)
mini marshmallows, to serve

Put the chocolate and sugar in a heavy-based saucepan. Pour in the milk, then add the vanilla extract and cinnamon.

Cover and gently heat, whisking once or twice, until the chocolate has melted. Continue heating until the mixture is steaming hot, but do not allow to boil. Stir in the Kahlua or other coffee liqueur, if liked.

Ladle the hot chocolate into 4 large cups or mugs and top with a few mini marshmallows. Serve immediately while steaming hot.

For peppermint hot chocolate, melt the chocolate in the milk as above, omitting the vanilla and cinnamon. Replace the coffee liqueur with 3 tablespoons peppermint liqueur, or for a non-alcoholic version use a couple of drops of good-quality natural peppermint extract instead. Divide the hot chocolate among 4 mugs, and top with swirls of freshly whipped cream or extra thick double cream, omitting the marshmallows. Hang a peppermint candy cane from the edge of each of the mugs for stirring and crunching and serve immediately.

banana & peanut butter smoothie

Serves **1**
Preparation time **10 minutes**,
  plus freezing

1 ripe **banana**
300 ml (½ pint) **semi-skimmed milk**
1 tablespoon **smooth peanut butter** or 2 teaspoons **tahini**

Peel and slice the banana, put it in a freezerproof container and freeze for at least 2 hours or overnight.

Put the banana, milk and peanut butter or tahini in a food processor or blender and process until smooth.

Pour the smoothie into a tall glass and serve immediately.

For banana almond smoothie, put 2 frozen bananas, 450 ml (¾ pint) soya milk, 40 g (1½ oz) ground almonds and a pinch of ground cinnamon in a food processor or blender. Process briefly until smooth.

the rehydrator

Serves **1**
Preparation time **10 minutes**

1 orange
50 g (2 oz) cucumber
100 ml (3½ fl oz) cranberry juice
ice cubes

Peel the orange, leaving on as much pith as possible. Using a juicer or blender, juice the orange and cucumber until smooth.

Mix the orange and cucumber juice with the cranberry juice, then pour into a tall glass over ice. Serve with cucumber stick stirrers.

For strawberry rehydrator, omit the cucumber and juice the orange with 250 g (8 oz) fresh strawberries. Mix with the cranberry juice and 1 teaspoon clear honey, blending or stirring until the honey has dissolved.

mind bath

Serves **1**
Preparation time **5 minutes**

100 g (3½ oz) **lettuce**, leaves
   torn or roughly chopped
½ **lemon**, peeled
100 ml (3½ fl oz) **chilled**
   camomile tea
ice cubes

Juice the lettuce and lemon using a juicer or blender until smooth.

Mix with the chilled camomile tea until well combined. Serve in a glass over ice.

For pear & ginger mind bath, omit the lettuce and juice 2 cored and quartered dessert pears and a 1.5 cm (½ inch) piece of peeled fresh root ginger until smooth. Mix with the chilled camomile tea.

index

acknowledgements

Executive Editor: Eleanor Maxfield
Editor: Joanne Wilson
Copy Editor: Siobhan O'Connor
Proofreader: Jo Richardson
Picture Manager: Jennifer Veall
Editorial Assistant: Diana Copeland
Senior Designer: Juliette Norsworthy
Design and Art Direction: Tracy Killick
Photographer: Stephen Conroy
Home economist: Sara Lewis

Props stylist: Kim Sullivan
Senior Production Controller: Caroline Alberti
Special photography: © Octopus Publishing Group
Limited/Stephen Conroy
Other photography: © Octopus Publishing/David
Munns 13, 39, 51, 53, 69, 97, 113, 141, 163, 171; Ian
Wallace 16-17, 101, 152-3, 182-3, 199; Lis Parsons 45,
103, 109, 131, 155, 169, 231; Sean Myers 165, 181;
Will Heap 5, 191, 197, 201, 213, 215; William Reavell
145; William Shaw 41, 193